NICK CLEMENTS

I SWEAR BY
ALMIGHTY
G-G-G-GOD

The politically incorrect memoirs of a police
officer who tried to make a difference

MEREO
Cirencester

Mereo Books

1A The Wool Market Dyer Street Cirencester Gloucestershire GL7 2PR
An imprint of Memoirs Publishing www.mereobooks.com

I Swear by Almighty G-G-G-God: 978-1-86151-771-5

First published in Great Britain in 2016
by Mereo Books, an imprint of Memoirs Publishing

The address for Memoirs Publishing Group Limited can be found at
www.memoirspublishing.com

The Memoirs Publishing Group Ltd Reg. No. 7834348

The Memoirs Publishing Group supports both The Forest Stewardship Council®
(FSC®) and the PEFC® leading international forest-certification organisations. Our
books carrying both the FSC label and the PEFC® and are printed on FSC®-certified
paper. FSC® is the only forest-certification scheme supported by the leading
environmental organisations including Greenpeace. Our paper procurement policy
can be found at www.memoirspublishing.com/environment

Typeset in 10/14pt Century Schoolbook
by Wiltshire Associates Publisher Services Ltd. Printed and bound in Great Britain
by Printondemand-Worldwide, Peterborough PE2 6XD

FOREWORD

These memoirs are not religious, despite the title. They are my memories of being an infant, child, teenager and young man in the 1950s and 60s, striving to escape from the wrong side of the tracks and a life dominated by my drunken, wife-beating, burgling, work-shy, narcissistic father. They are an accurate account of my unrelenting ambition to become a police officer, despite these obstacles and a stutter to boot. The memories of my childhood are, mostly, sad.

Memories of my police career began as a police cadet in the 1960s, not long after leaving school, no qualifications, at the tender age of fifteen, and with a stutter. 'God', 'Nick', 'bread and butter,' were my staple stumbling blocks to conversations and as a policeman, giving evidence. My memories of the politically-incorrect decades of the sixties, seventies and eighties are rich with anecdotes of horror, humour, fear, fun, passion, sex, marriages, excitement, commendations and above all, the determination to escape my past and make a future. If you are of a nervous disposition, put this book back on the shelf now!

I continuously reached for the stars. I never actually reached them, but I was over the moon – as they say – with the progress I made and the stubbornness that got me there. I had children, promotions and three marriages. I not only survived, but thrived. Think of this as 'Billy Elliott' meets 'The Sweeney', and you'll have the gist of it.

CONTENTS

1

A DAD WHO DIDN'T DESERVE THE NAME

Having a dad – for want of a better word – who was a wife-beater, a drunk, a thief, a burglar and an idle, lazy, work-shy, vain, narcissistic egotist encouraged me to start work early and contribute to the family's basic need for food and rent. One abiding memory of acute embarrassment is of going to primary school in summer wearing wellingtons because my shoes had so many holes they were flapping at the front and sole. Crying all the way there, and crying even harder when the usual suspects gloated and pointed out my situation to everyone else, running home, still crying, to sit in the shed next to the coal house, until I was rescued by my mam. Leaving school earlier than most and starting a job, not a career, to earn some money seemed to me the right thing to do to help my Mam and siblings.

How Mam and I often cried together when she told me he'd found the rent money she'd hidden, again, and gone off to the pub, again. How I hated him! Why couldn't he just go to work like all the other dads in our street? That question was the most common one asked by Mam and I when we were in despair. So starting work earlier than my friends really wasn't an option; it seemed to me a necessity.

Although I took a job as an apprentice fitter at a local engineering factory, my dream from as far back as I could remember was to be a policeman. I was asked the same question as everyone else. 'What do you want to be when you grow up?' 'A policeman,' I always replied. I suppose policemen were my role models in my early life, given that they were more frequent visitors to our house than relatives. Whenever they took my dad away for a stint in prison we would have some tranquillity or relief for a time; a bit of happiness and laughter.

When I say we, I include my siblings. My sister Margaret was born four years after me, my brother Gary four years after her, another sister, Gaynor, three years after Gary and another sister, Lisa, two years after that. Katherine, my stepsister, arrived after my mam was finally divorced, and long after I'd left home at the tender age of sixteen. I remember overhearing my mam telling my auntie that she didn't think she'd ever had sex with my dad when he was sober. Funny how you remember little comments, but looking back, that probably explains a lot.

So how would it be possible for a 16-year-old with my background to become a police cadet? How many stumbling blocks could there be? I had no qualifications, but I was exceptionally honest, hard-working and protective of my mother, grandmother and anyone who was weak or bullied – particularly female. 'Old beyond my years,' I heard many people say, but that was mainly down to trying to be a role model to my siblings, including shielding them from the drunken loutish behaviour of their dad whenever I could, and doing the shopping at the local Co-op every day. I was always first at the local paper shop waiting for the owner to open up and give me my sacks to distribute, seven days a week morning and evening, for the princely sum – in today's money – of 75 pence per week. And more often than not I bought food with it.

But I knew my biggest problem would be my stutter. I struggled with my surname because it began with the letter C. It was the same with 'bread and butter' and, of course, 'God', although He wasn't someone I referred to regularly, prior to joining the police service. There would be quite a few "Gs" before finally the word 'God!' exploded from my stammering lips, but I wasn't to know that, until I was being trained how to give the Oath, with one hand on the Bible, in a witness box, in front of my peers. 'I swear by Almighty… ' Almost as embarrassing as going to school in wellies. But that comes later. And, for fellow stutterers, some great tips on how to stop stuttering!

And yet my new life as a police cadet nearly stopped just after it started.

2

A POST MORTEM, EVIL MEN AND AN APOLOGY

This is what can happen when you put yourself on a pedestal and believe with absolute sincerity that your life is on the way up. You can easily get knocked off. This happened in spectacular fashion about three months into my career as a cadet, as I'd now started referring to it, and it could so easily have been the end of that career. It started at the divisional headquarters of Derbyshire Constabulary, in Matlock.

One particular sergeant had obviously taken a dislike to me, when almost everyone else seemed to have taken a bit of a shine to me. Some of my superiors were by now referring to me as 'lad' or 'Nick', and said they had often seen me swimming up and down the local pool like a fish. I played snooker with quite a few of them in meal breaks and after work. But this one sadist, Sergeant Johnson, seemed to snarl at me whenever he asked me to do something or questioned me about what I had done. I was always very respectful towards him, but quite frankly I was scared to death of him. I don't mind being disrespectful about him now, he'll be long dead, and I would describe him as an ugly chain smoker with brown uneven teeth and bad breath. I did hear another sergeant tell him to leave me alone as I was doing all right, but it didn't improve his attitude towards me.

This particular day, referring to me as Cadet 8, he asked me if I'd seen a post-mortem. It wasn't really a question, more of a statement, because obviously I hadn't. How many 16-year-olds had even seen a dead body? I knew there was a mortuary exactly opposite our police station and I'd often seen ambulances and plain vans driving round the back of it from the window where my desk was. No one had ever discussed the term 'post mortem' with me, let alone prepared me for one and what it entailed. Until recently, I'd been more into Workers' Playtime on the radio, in the company of my mam and the Daleks in Doctor Who – watching through slatted fingers from behind the settee at my friend's house.

It was quite apparent that he'd organised something, because a minute later he told me to get up and put my jacket and cap on, I was going to see one. As I walked through the office I heard the civilian switchboard operator call him a bastard, and it wasn't long before I was thinking the same. I walked across the road with him and he unlocked the big heavy brass hinged door at the front of the mortuary and we went in together. It was like a very big garage; concrete floor painted cream, brick walls painted cream, very bright, and very cold. As we entered I saw a couple of long, smooth stone tables on blocks of stone, with shallow curves towards the centre down the length of them, and a hole at one end leading to a drain hole in the floor. They were like large static operating tables, but concave instead of flat. There was a large writing bureau in a small office and some large steel cabinets along one wall, where I presumed the bodies were stored.

Despite its cleanliness, tidiness and brightness, it was characterless and absolutely uninviting. Mind you, what mortuary would be inviting?

The sergeant grabbed my right arm and pulled me round a corner, then pulled harder when I stopped. Lying on a sheet of tin on top of a stone table was the body of a woman in her twenties or thirties. She was completely naked, with small breasts and a lot of pubic hair. There was nothing sexual about that first sight of a naked woman.

The Bastard Sergeant pulled me harder, until we were in front of the body and standing on a wooden platform, presumably there to stop your feet from freezing over. My eyes were torn between staring at her and up at the ceiling. I heard him reminding me that I was a police cadet and would be seeing a lot of dead bodies and I had better get used to it.

I nearly jumped out of my skin when the pathologist, it couldn't have been anyone else, suddenly appeared on my other side. He looked as if he'd stepped out of a Boris Karloff film. He was about a foot shorter than me, almost bald, with milk-bottle glasses that made his eyes look as though they were on stalks, and wearing a heavy-duty rubber apron and rubber gloves. His bottom lip protruded. I'd never heard the word 'malevolent', but now that I'm more worldly-wise, that's how I would describe his appearance.

The Bastard Sergeant told him I was Cadet 8 and I was here to watch a post-mortem. He said he would be back in half an hour or so. Who should I be most afraid of, I asked myself, the living or the dead? I know he asked me some questions, and I know I was unable to speak. He leaned across the woman, telling me she was quite dead. Her eyes were closed. He lifted her left arm up and it creaked and stayed up almost vertical, leaning against the far wall. Then, mercifully, he rolled out a leather bag, containing all sorts of metal instruments, including scalpels, spoons and a small tenon saw, across the top of her legs, covering her private parts. That definitely helped. He told me he was going to open her body. His finger pointed to her throat, where he was going to cut, down to her stomach. He would, he said, saw either side of her rib cage and lift it up to see inside her chest.

I know he took delight in explaining that he would insert the scalpel he was holding into the bottom of her neck, cut down and then peel back her skin. I was transfixed. I still hadn't spoken a word. I was shivering and sweating at the same time and I wanted to put my hand on the stone table to stop myself from swaying, but I didn't. I just stood there mesmerised, frightened and feeling childish. Exactly the opposite of what a police cadet should be doing, presumably.

It was pure theatre, or more like pure horror. He laid the scalpel on her breast and took out a packet of Capstan Full Strength cigarettes and lit one. He left it dangling from his lips, picked the scalpel up and just stuck it in the bottom of her throat. She exhaled loudly and her arm dropped from vertical to crash against the sheet of tin. The noise was deafening.

My next recollection was dodging the traffic as I ran across the road into the police station foyer. I was fumbling with the coded access buttons trying to get in when the Bastard Sergeant opened it, grabbed my arm and pulled me back out of the station, shouting things like, 'what do you think you're doing?', 'where's your cap?', 'you're a disgrace', as he dragged me back across the road towards the mortuary door. I kept shouting, 'she's alive, she's alive!'

Suddenly I was on the wooden platform again, my right arm held tightly as the pathologist walked from his desk to us. He showed no emotion as he lit another Capstan full strength from the stub of the previous one and dropped that on the floor. I normally hated the smell of cigarettes, but I wasn't aware of anything other than watching him pick up the scalpel from where he had left it between her breasts.

The next half hour was a blur. He cut her open, peeled back her skin and flesh across and under her breasts, and then used his saw to cut down the side of her rib cage. Mercifully, in some respects, when he pulled her rib cage up it covered her face. He spoke through the haze of cigarette smoke as he pulled body parts out of the cavity, weighed them and put them in separate metal dishes on a nearby mobile table. I noticed that the Bastard Sergeant had gone, but at what point I had no idea. I was stupefied with fear and horror, concentrating on keeping my own bile inside my body and hoping against hope I wouldn't fall over.

Mr Malevolent chain-smoked throughout, lighting each new fag from the old one. When he told me he was going to examine her brain he asked me to stand next to him. I couldn't move or speak and watched as the top of her head was pulled over from back to front to hide her eyes and heard him sawing the top of her head off. I went into a trance, I think, and just stood there as he weighed, made notes, examined bits and pieces and smoked.

I think I could have lived with my experience and moved

on if I had witnessed only the post-mortem, bearing in mind what I would witness in years to come. But the way she breathed out and her arm fell down continues to this day to haunt my dreams and nightmares.

It was ten years later, as a seasoned detective in drugs squad, when the vision again came to mind and it dawned on me that I had been set up by the two of them. They knew that the build-up of gases inside her body would create the exhalation noise when the hole was made in her neck, and the release of that pressure would also cause her arm to fall down. Their little game was designed to create the effect it had on me. Bastards.

At least recognising what they had done, at last, helped me come to terms with my demons. What I should have done was talk about what had happened instead of keeping my silence. Not for the purpose of recriminations, but telling friends might have lessened the immediate effect it had on me. Perhaps someone might even have spotted the malicious "trick" they had played.

But, all that said, there is no way I can move on from the pathologist's final act. Even as I write this, my blood boils in anger. I'm ashamed of myself, at my lack of action then and subsequently. My own inadequacies come to the fore every time I recollect what he did. I should have grabbed the pathologist by the throat, or at the very least, spoken up of the injustice, abuse and the malfeasance I witnessed, when, as he was sewing up her body he spat his final cigarette into her cavity. His final words to me were, 'It doesn't matter to her, she's dead.'

When the Bastard Sergeant came for me I know he held my arm as we walked across the road with him stopping the traffic. I was in the toilet for so long there was nothing left in my stomach other than pain. I don't remember talking to anyone in the station afterwards, but one of the older officers came and sat with me and asked if I was going to be okay. He definitely said, 'He's a bastard!' Looking back, I don't know if he was referring to the sergeant or the pathologist.

I have silently apologised to that woman's family thousands of times since, and still do. If only I could turn back the clock and have an opportunity to change just one thing in my life, I would defend her decency in a forceful way. That experience, together with memories of my own mother's treatment, certainly paved the way for my future unswerving need to stand up for justice and speak out against injustice, particularly where that involved women and girls. But my personal shame, created by my inactivity that day, remains.

I never told anyone at work, or any of my friends, about my experience. I thought of it as part of my training and my daily life continued, if rather subdued for a while. But my nightlife changed dramatically, without my knowledge. My landlady asked me numerous times over the next few weeks what was wrong as she heard me screaming out in my sleep. Of course my memory of that day was indelible and I did know sometimes I was having nightmares about it, but she told me I was screaming every night and she was concerned.

It must have been very disconcerting for my landlady's family, because she reported her concerns to the Chief Inspector of Cadets. I didn't know at the time that she had done that. Out of the blue, it seemed to me, he called my extension and asked me to come up to his office. Although I was fearful of anyone in authority at this time, I was always pleased to see him when he walked through the office, rather as a Labrador looks at his master, I suspect. I saluted smartly and anticipated our first in-depth talk about swimming and life-saving training. Instead he told me he was sending me home for a week, that I should enjoy the rest and consider talking to a doctor about my nightmares. He never mentioned my visit to the mortuary.

I had by this time bought one of the oldest 125cc motorbikes in existence, similar in appearance to the ones used in the war, with just the one seat shaped like a large pedal cycle seat. I had goggles but no helmet. I went home first, anticipating going on to stay with my grandma after spending some time with my siblings. But Mam had received a letter from the Chief Inspector of Cadets and she asked me to stay the night and said she wanted to talk to me about what I had been up to. Mam and I had always talked and even laughed together during my school days and I had no problem accepting her invitation, even though our relationship had become slightly strained since I had left home.

The very next morning she told me she had to take me to the doctor's. She said I shouldn't be screaming like that in my sleep and she went with me to the surgery in Clay Cross, our nearest town. There was no appointment made in those days, you just sat and waited your turn. Like the time I told my mam I'd been weeing blood. I'd flushed the toilet so there was no evidence, but she made me drink glasses of water until I could go again. She watched, told me to hold it, got a milk bottle and I half filled it with bloodied urine. We went straight to the doctors, after waiting at the bus stop for ages and then waiting all over again in the queue at the surgery, me panicking and my mam apparently stoic. Two minutes after showing the doctor my blood sample, I was told to cut down on the beetroot sandwiches.

This time my mam came into the surgery with me, but after she had told the doctor about my noisy sleeping habits,

I asked her to wait outside, as I wanted to talk to the doctor confidentially. I told him some of what had happened, but most importantly I missed the opportunity to explain all the details and bring the Boris Karloff pathologist to justice.

The doctor called my mother in and asked me to wait outside this time. When we left I had some tablets to take. My mother was very thoughtful, suggesting I stayed with her and not at my grandma's as I might frighten her during the night. I don't recollect my dad being there at this juncture. I took the tablets for two nights, threw the rest of them in the bin and went back to my digs, after only three nights away. I believed I should be stronger and didn't want a blemish on my record. I would live with my issue and sleep with it. I was sure I could stop myself from screaming and upsetting people during the night. I asked my landlady after a couple of nights if I had woken anyone up, and she said the tablets must be working.

There was a very noticeable change though. As a consequence of my experience my stutter was back, with a vengeance. Not just back, but worse than before. I knew I could and would conquer it though. I had to be a successful police cadet, if not the brightest. I had to. I could not fail. I was still in my cadetship probationary period and I knew I couldn't afford to be seen as unsuitable, in either attitude or commitment.

My decision to go back to work earlier than I was supposed to was not based on reasoning, or better health; it was more intuitive. Throughout my life I have never really spent much time thinking and planning my future, short or long term. My actions have always been the result of instinct, rapidly implemented with enthusiasm, before I have had time to counsel myself to be cautious. This was something I have never practised; it just happens that way, and I'm thankful for it. I would never have applied to join the police cadets if I'd reasoned with myself or procrastinated, or taken advice from my family or friends – or girlfriend. I would never have progressed in my career if I'd waited until I was sure that what I was attempting to achieve was achievable. And I certainly wouldn't have been awarded so many Crown Court and Chief Constable commendations if I'd faltered for a second, or thought of the consequences of making a mistake.

I don't know who passed these genes down to me, but thanks anyway. They seem to have worked, at least on Pareto's Principle of eighty-twenty, so far. To save some of you Googling Pareto's Principle, or Pareto's Law, it is a well-established description of averages. Examine any troubles you have. Eighty per cent of your problems at home or work are caused by twenty per cent of your staff. The idea is to concentrate on the twenty per cent to simplify improving your life. In many cases eighty per cent of things just happen and are achieved without planning and forethought – but that twenty per cent can catch you out. The same applies in the police service too. More often than not, eighty per cent of the crime in an area will be committed by twenty per cent of the criminal fraternity. So concentrate your efforts on the prolific ones – the twenty per cent – using a smaller group of officers rather than more officers chasing everyone.

When I went back to work I noticed a subtle change in my colleagues' attitude towards me. The atmosphere was friendlier, and more people involved me in conversations. There were more snooker opportunities and the two other cadets who joined with me even asked if they could come swimming with me and asked if I would teach them life-saving techniques. I liked to think it was my personality that had won them over, but I soon realised it was because the Bastard Sergeant had moved to another police station during my short, but enforced, time off work. I wasn't the only person in the station who was pleased.

No one ever asked me about my post-mortem experience and I never talked about it to anyone. It was a shameful omission on my part not to stand up for that poor woman and her family, but if the Bastard Sergeant had been moved because of what he'd done to me, the pathologist should have been rotting in hell. But should a 16-year-old youth, I reasoned, police cadet or otherwise, have to consider wielding that amount of destructive power, affecting the futures of "superior" men in higher places, and their unwitting families? I took the easy option I suppose and have lived to regret my inadequacy. The lady and her family will never know of course – but for my own peace of mind at last, please let this be my apology in writing.

3

A WIFE-BEATING, DRUNKEN WASTER

But let me explain how I managed to become a police cadet in the first place, and talk about the hurdles I needed to overcome, and the luck that helped. Being the son of a miner (and I use that description loosely, as my 'dad' spent more time in the pub propping up the bar than he did propping a mineshaft), I was also the relative of many other miners. I was obviously expected to go down that route – or, rather, that mine. But I recall having the mindset from an early age, probably about five, that I would never follow in his footsteps. Having a dad who was the antithesis of an upstanding hard-working family man, I would never be a miner because I would never be like him.

From that age onwards, I also remember him being

asleep on the settee stinking of beer after a session in the pub, or prior to going back to the pub. My mam and I would keep out of his way when he woke up if he was looking anything like angry or nasty. Too often he would shout, threaten and violently demand the rent money. He would search her purse, handbag and cupboards, shouting and swearing and threatening her until eventually he would, literally, throttle her into submission and she would go to a hiding place and give him some of the money. If only he knew that I was always privy to the different places where my mam hid the money. I would have submitted far more easily than she did. We were close to eviction so many times. How many times did we hide under the stairs when the rent man came to collect something that was being spent in the pub? 'Dad' would whistle and sing and clean his shoes with his slippers and tell me with a wink that the sign of a good lover is clean shoes. Once he'd got his hands on the rent money he swaggered to the pub, leaving my mam with bruises and little money for food, sitting on a chair with her head in her hands crying. It wouldn't be long before I was sent to a neighbour with a cup to borrow some sugar or milk for a cup of tea and, as many times as I came back without any, I was sent to another, further down the road, always mindful of missing out the ones I had already borrowed from that week.

My worst memories stem from his being at the pub during the day and then coming back again at night. We were guaranteed to be in for a nasty and violent night that invariably ended up with my police officer role models taking him away for assaulting my mam or being drunk and disorderly. I was an avid reader of books borrowed from the local library, and my favourites were the Jennings and Darbishire books of humorous schoolboy adventures. I have some fantastic memories of sitting on the settee next to my mam in front of the coal fire reading by candlelight and sharing out loud some of the funnier passages, which had us both hysterical with laughter. Then we would hear him coming up the path shouting some ribald comment to one of his mates and we would pray he would go straight to bed without coming into the room where we were. We sat and waited in fear.

Remember, when I was five I had a one-year-old sister and when I was nine, we both had a brother aged one. At various times, depending on how my 'dad' behaved in drink, the night could be filled with a cacophony of noise with my mam screaming in agony from black eyes, broken noses and fingers and massive bruises from his fist and feet attacks, plus the higher-pitched screaming and wailing of one to three children. First the neighbouring men would come round and pull him off my mam, followed by their wives to put us back into bed and sit with us as we waited for my role models to come and arrest him, or if mam had to be taken to hospital.

Sometimes I would have the company of a neighbour all night if Mam was taken to hospital, but more times than I can remember I was left in charge of the house and my sister and brother for hours at a time. I still have nightmares about feeding my one-year-old brother with a spoon, as he sat in his wooden high chair in the living room, when my dad started on my mam. I left my brother for literally seconds to close the kitchen door to reduce the noise and he slid out of the chair because I hadn't strapped him. He fell onto the floor and his head caught the tiled hearth. There was blood everywhere. Not only did he have a nasty scar on his forehead when he came out of hospital, he still had it 50-odd years later. Not that we've ever talked about it. I was in horrific shock at the sight of all the blood and him crying and I've been in denial ever since. It did however rescue my mam from the other ordeal, temporarily.

I wasn't a fan of my sister and brother in the early days, mainly because of imposed baby-sitting duties. I didn't have a problem in the house, but when my brother was about a year old and still in a pram, I was forced to take him and my five-year-old sister when I went out to play with my gang. She would hold the side of the pram, while he was invariably asleep as I joined my mates to race around to the estate park half a mile away.

I had to join in, despite my encumbrances, because I was joint leader of our gang, the Black Hand Gang. Members of the gang had to rub the charcoal from a burnt stick on their left palm before we set off. No black hand, no membership. So I treated the pram as a racing car and chased around the hurdles and obstacles created by playground furniture or used it as part of a wagon train whilst the rest of the gang played Cowboys and Indians. My sister obviously wasn't a member, being just a girl, but she was normally content to play on the swings on her own. We only went home when it became apparent it was baby-feeding time.

I don't have many solid memories of my younger family. I've thought about this a lot over the years, and particularly during this writing, and I can only believe that subconsciously I've blocked those times and memories out of my life. It's a bit late to see a psychiatrist now, but I do believe that's what I've done. My memory is clouded about the births of the five children who followed me. I have some recollections of my mam going to hospital in ambulances, but I don't know for sure if she was off to give birth or be treated in A&E for husband-inflicted injuries. I have only one memory of being alone with my dad, and that still makes me shudder. I do know I could have and should have been a better brother, but I can't change that. I can't even turn the clock back to any particular incidents of shared love or even shared pain – other than the nightmare when we were locked in the bedroom together. There were certainly no picnics, holidays or shopping trips as a family. I don't remember any birthday parties for any of us. I do remember getting a two-wheeled bike for Christmas once and my dad asking me to go to the Co-op and get him ten Park Drive fags on it. It was to be my first journey on it and I didn't want to do it because I was so anti-smoking and anti-him. I remember the two incidents, the new bike and shopping for fags for him, each as memorable as the other.

I also remember seeing my Uncle Gordon walking from the bus stop towards our house carrying a home-made sledge and trying to hide it wrapped in a plastic sheet. At that point in my life I was a bit sceptical about Santa Claus. My suspicions were confirmed when the sledge was at the bottom of my bed on Christmas Day. I also remember it didn't snow enough to use it that winter. We always had a sock pinned at the bottom of the bed with an apple, an orange and some nuts in their shells. I hope there were some good things that happened in my life as a young child and Christmases were actually better than I've described, but I honestly can't remember. My life was about surviving for a future, even though I certainly didn't know it then. I also wish fervently that I had more and better memories. So, sorry to my brother and sisters.

My posh best friend, Neil, from across the road, was never allowed to join our gang or be out with us. I either played with him, just the two of us, or I played with the rough lads in our gang. There were two very different types of culture and behaviour. My choice was Black Hand Gang or a two-man cricket match, unless it was night time and then it was a choice between climbing lampposts and throwing each other into privet hedges and bouncing back out, or indoor lessons on how to play Monopoly and Scrabble, supervised by Neil's mum. What my mam did during these times I'm not sure, but I have my suspicions.

I've only written a few pages and its already preying on my mind that I've used the word "dad" about half a dozen times and I'm concerned how many more times I'll have to use it. I intend, and I hope you will too, if you continue reading, to imagine that word is just that – a reference word – and not a reference to a father figure, and particularly not my father. If the word dad changes as you read to "bad" it will not be a typing mistake, just a better description.

I've already explained why I had to wear wellies to school for a period of time and the acute embarrassment they caused me. I also have a more vivid memory of wearing wellies when my mam was in hospital, either giving birth to my brother or because my dad had badly beaten her.

It was my job to make the fire every morning and get the house, oven and water warm before anyone else got up. I was quite good at this; lighting rolled up newspapers under the free coal we got, then holding the shovel in front of the fire with a broad sheet of newspaper across it pressed to the sides of the fireplace with one hand and a foot, my spare hand holding the shovel handle. This helped the fire to draw and as the paper started to scorch, just before it caught fire, I would let go of it and it would disappear in a whoosh of flame up the chimney. I got a pleasant feeling of achievement from seeing the fire going, but on this particular morning I realised I didn't have any shoes to go to school in and my mood changed. I found my plastic sandals under the stairs and put them on just as my dad came downstairs. I could hear my sister crying upstairs.

As I left the house he pulled me back in and told me I couldn't go to school in sandals, as it was too cold. I can remember the discussion as I cried and told him that I didn't have any shoes and the sandals were fine. Probably making his first-ever decision involving his children's welfare, he told me to wear wellingtons. I wasn't and am still not fashion conscious, but wellies and short trousers on a dry day would make me the laughing stock of the primary school, again. I lost the discussion because he was not a person to argue with, so I did my usual and cried all the way to school, during school and on my way back home.

However, I went one better on this occasion, and in between my sobs of self-consciousness, I shat myself when I was about half way home. I drew attention to myself just running in wellies, but with the brown stuff running down the back of my legs into the wellies, I was a sight to remember. I ran bow-legged, howling and shrugging off a woman who tried to hug me as she was walking her son and friend of mine home from school. I remember getting a slap on my leg from my dad when I got in for being in such a state, but he was careful to waggle me around so he could choose a spot where his hand didn't get dirty.

4

ALMOST A MURDERER

██▼█▼█▼█▼█▼█▼█▼█▼█▼█▼█▼█▼█

I like to think I got my own back on my 'dad' in a small way
– although I only think of this now and didn't at the time.

In the early hours of one morning my mother's
screaming and his shouting followed by crashing furniture
was particularly bad. I lay in bed listening and waiting for
the neighbours to burst in, but it went unusually quiet. I
went to the top of the stairs and heard sounds I hadn't heard
before – gurgling and gasping noises. I knew this was
serious, or more serious than the other beatings, because
prior to the silence this beating had been very violent. I
couldn't stop myself going downstairs to see how bad it was.
He was kneeling over her and gnashing his teeth, with his
hands round my mam's neck. His face was contorted and
her eyes were bulging out and I instinctively knew he was
killing her. I jumped on his back and started pulling his hair

and screaming. I can still remember how slick his hair was with Brylcreem, so I couldn't get a proper hold.

I don't know what made me think of it, because there was nothing in the house I could have used to hit him with, without going out to the coal house for the shovel, but I knew that the handle on the door between the room they were in and the kitchen was missing and the square metal bolt the handles turned on was exposed. In an inspired move I got off him and pulled the bolt out of the door – all four inches of it – and started to poke it into his face and head as hard as I could, still screaming at the top of my voice for help. He had to let go with one hand from her throat to swat me away, and as soon as I got up I attacked him again.

The neighbours pulled me off him first, and then him off my mam, then the police took him away and the ambulance took my mam away. That incident was very serious and my mam had black, blue, maroon and yellow finger marks on her neck and black eyes for ages. He was in prison for a while after that episode and our lives were tranquil for a short time, although I shared Mam's fear of no money, little food and plenty of borrowing from relatives and neighbours.

At around this time, I remember accompanying my mam to the pit head office, two bus rides away, where she was crying and begging for money and coal to people in the offices. I remember her squeezing my hand as she pulled me from one office to another trying to find a manager who would listen. I had quite a few days off school to do these kinds of visits with my mam, or to help look after my siblings when she went on her own, or if she was ill or heavily pregnant and needed my presence at home. There was no welfare state then, or not like the one we have today, just good neighbours and resourcefulness. The neighbours, particularly the women, must have been thinking, 'But for the Grace of God...'.

If I wanted to watch television as a child in the 1950s I would have to wait until my best friend Neil's mam and dad asked me in. They lived opposite us. His dad was a lovely man. He was a miner who smoked a pipe and spent a lot of his time in his wonderful garden; a well-tended lawn and loads of flowers in the front and loads of vegetables in the back. He worked down the pit and the blue scars on his face and backs of his hands proved it. He always came home clean though, not like mine. On the odd occasion mine did go to work he would come home dirty from coal dust, lie on the settee smelly and with dirty feet and toe nails. He was repugnant.

My best mate's mum was a Cockney. His parents met in the war and he brought his wife up north to get married. She was such a happy person, always busy cooking and cleaning and very houseproud. I'm not sure if she ever spoke to my parents, but every now and then she would ask me to come in when I called to play with Neil. I was allowed to wait in their kitchen if he was finishing his piano lessons or his homework, and she would ask me to help shell peas and broad beans from their garden. Our garden had never even seen a spade and you could play hide-and-seek in the massive weeds and long grass. It was simply two different worlds – our street of well-kept council houses occupied in the main by proud-but-poor pit workers, with ours looking like an overgrown tip. My view of their house, from ours, was lovely.

Sometimes in the winter when it was too cold and dark for the two of us to be playing cricket using their lamp post for the stumps, Neil's mum would invite me in to watch their TV. It was black and white of course, and minute by today's standards. Even though I was invited to sit next to my mate on their settee (his mum called it a sofa!) I knew the state of my clothing and I insisted on sitting on the floor near the door, with my balaclava on. She would tell me to take it off, but she didn't know that I'd had, and might still have, nits. So I sweltered in front of a roaring coal fire, drinking tea with only my eyes on show, but I loved being there. I stayed the night once, top and tail with Neil, in his crisp clean bed, but only after I'd had a bath and been given a pair of his underpants (mine were put in their dustbin). I slept in a pair of his pyjamas. No overcoats on the bed either. It was heaven, and I owe his mum and my mate a debt of gratitude for allowing me an insight into what a hard-working, friendly and loving family life can provide. Unwittingly at the time, it was something that helped me to aspire to a different life.

Nothing stops you loving your mam and wanting to protect her, but if you don't experience something that opens your eyes to a better life, you might grow up thinking your own life was normal and adjust to it naturally. When I look back I recognise that staying the night in their clean and loving house was my first step, psychologically, to moving away from my own.

Neil's mum and dad came to my siblings' rescue and mine one summer evening. How many people have had a nightmare over 50 years earlier which stills plays over and over? I remember clearly waking up from one of my nightmares screaming and sweating and panicking. It was still light and my young sister and younger brother were sitting on my bed crying. They had discovered that the bedroom door was locked and their screaming and panic became hysterical when no one responded. I leaned out of my bedroom window, shouting that we were alone and locked in. We must have looked a sight, with me screaming and frightened and my sister and brother standing on the window sill, both howling.

Neil and his parents were walking home from church and saw us, so it must have been a Sunday evening. I heard them banging on our door. Obviously we were alone, so Neil's dad went to his house and brought a ladder back. Someone must have contacted the police, and they arrived just as he was climbing into the bedroom. Our house became the focal point for half the street. Then a police car turned up with my mam in the back. She'd been at the pub with my dad, and I remember the sergeant shouting at her and her crying. I don't remember the outcome, but I do know my dad wasn't there; he'd obviously stayed in the pub. This incident above many others recurs in my sleeping and waking life, like a trauma.

My wonderful grandparents, on my mother's side, lived about five miles away from us; two bus rides, or more often than not a one-mile walk and a bus ride to get there. They were lovely. Granddad was always whistling. He had a full head of hair, but it was shockingly white. They both spoke to me gently, always, and I even remember my granddad shouting at my mam for something she'd done to make me cry, rescuing me from the bottom step of the staircase to the bedrooms. I can't remember what I'd done, or what my mam had done to me, but she stormed off, leaving me in the comfort of their company. I always enjoyed being at their house with them, especially when their next-door neighbour gave me a wind-up record player, although it had only one record, of *Smoke Gets In Your Eyes*, which I played repeatedly. Eventually, even my grandparents' patience gave in and I had to play it in the back yard, not in their house. I well remember the open fire with the black oven built into the side of the chimney and a metal grille that swung over the fire so the kettle could be boiled, or swung to the side to keep it simmering. And of course the bread that came out of that oven. I was always given a good thick slice of crust as soon as it came out, the butter melting even as it got near the bread. Now, *they* are happy memories!

The number of times my mother packed a suitcase and took me – and later my sister and me and later still my brother, sister and me – to live with my grandparents when she was in fear of her life were too frequent for me to be accurate about the years. I know on two occasions I started at their nearby primary school for weeks at a time, only to be later repatriated to the matrimonial home, and back to my local primary and junior school.

I can't remember the question a schoolteacher at my new occasional school asked me, but I remember not knowing the answer and looking dumb. He threw the wooden blackboard rubber at me, caught me on the top of my head as I ducked and knocked me out of the chair. He came over and picked the rubber up and started chanting at me 'scatterbrain, scatterbrain!'. The chant was continued by the children in the playground for the weeks I was there. Unusually for me, I think, I didn't have a friend to turn to at this school.

I know I went back to this terrible school a second time, after my mam had been assaulted and ended up in hospital, but I do believe that in the interests of my future self-preservation I blocked out the memories of my time there this time. I did though, build up a particularly close and loving relationship with my grandma in this period of my life and would regularly spend weekends at their house. I can remember going to sleep in the spare room but always waking up in bed with the two of them.

This was preferable for me, despite there only being an outside toilet shared with spiders and squares of newspaper hung on a piece of wire. And of course the tin bath in front of the fire, but it was good enough for my grandma and granddad, so it was good enough for me. One of the main reasons I hated my mam's house – apart from 'him' being in it – was overflowing ash trays and all the fag ends lined up on every ledge in the house, including the inside bathroom and toilet, where they had burnt down and turned the paint brown. Did I have the potential at this time to be a selfish, spoiled brat? I think there was a little of this, as I was always angry and embarrassed at having to stand up every morning – at both schools – and say out loud in class that I was on free school dinners. There was always me, sometimes two of us, but it was always the worst possible start to my school day. All the other kids paid the five shillings a week, or was it two and six? It was my constant shame and humiliation, because my father was a drunk and wouldn't go to work. But it was always much worse for my mam.

All this before I was eleven, before I failed my Eleven-Plus exam, before starting secondary school – and before I even knew I had a stutter. And my poor grandma, Ada. She lost my granddad, Jim, when I was about nine or ten. I remember being grabbed by a very large, buxom, motherly woman, whose son I knew vaguely, as I walked home from junior school one day. She nearly suffocated me as she told me I was to stay at her house for a few hours, as my granddad had died suddenly and my mam had gone to see my grandma. I don't remember anything else about his death, but I carried on visiting my grandma as usual.

5

PRIMARY SCHOOL MEMORIES
AND A BOOK ON BIRDS

▪▪▪▪▪▪▪▪▪▪▪▪▪▪▪▪▪▪

I know my saving grace was sport. I was able to swim and run forever. I never had any football boots, for obvious reasons, so I never played that game. When I left Holmgate Primary School to go to the big school in Clay Cross, I believe the infant teachers there would have remembered me for three reasons. The first reason would be my last afternoon at the end of the last term. Everyone was in the assembly room, most kids with a parent or two, but not mine. Parents sat on chairs and kids sat cross-legged on the floor. I was absolutely amazed when my name was called out for being the school's best-ever swimmer. I had an unbelievable sense of joy and pride. The headmistress and our local councillor presented me with a Ladybird book on garden birds, to what I thought was rapturous and ecstatic applause. I left that school for the last time and ran home clutching the book, which I showed my mam straightaway. I told her what had happened and she read the book with me for ages. It was on my bedroom windowsill every day until I left home, so I could identify every bird that had the temerity to enter our pigsty of a garden.

The local councillor and her son lived diagonally opposite our house and we all knew them as posh; they only ever spoke to Neil's mum and dad. A manicured yellow and green privet hedge surrounded the front of their house, with a locked gate to the path where her son kept his motorbike and sidecar. Whenever one of our balls went into their garden she would take it indoors, and we would never get it back. If her son was there he would use his penknife to puncture it and then throw it back. Theirs was a garden to avoid at all costs when playing football in the street and the occupiers were to be avoided even more so, wherever they were.

The local constable stopped me in the street and told me off after the one and only time I'd been brave enough to climb their gate to retrieve a ball, thinking they were out. In those days you didn't do something wrong twice. But on this memorable end-of-school day, the councillor stood up and shook my hand in front of the whole school when she gave me the book. She smiled and told me I'd done well and hoped I would be successful at my new school. After that she always smiled and said hello to me, using my first name, when she saw me in the street. I, and my mates, always thought of her as an ogre and we were frightened of her, but she made me feel very proud and after that I could only admire her.

The second reason I would be remembered at my school was for falling down a complete flight of stairs, from top to bottom, at the head of the stampede to get out of school at going home time, snapping one of my two front teeth in half. I was taken to the headmistress's study and a nurse was called for. When I was shown the result in a mirror, with half a tooth in my hand, I was told I was very brave for not crying. In truth there was no pain, but I was hailed as a bit of a hero for a few weeks, even though I couldn't smile about it.

The third reason I would be remembered, by the teachers only, hopefully, would have been embarrassing if I had known then what I know now. I climbed the climbing frame in the playground all the time and was quite an acrobat. One day I realised that if I gripped the tallest pole by wrapping my legs round it and slid slowly from top to bottom, the friction this created on my willy was extremely pleasant. I would repeat this process throughout the breaks and I was in heaven, without understanding or knowing the cause and effect. This pleasurable activity continued regularly, until one of the lady teachers told me to stop climbing the frame. She didn't say anything other than 'Stop climbing the frame'. But I'd become addicted to the pleasure, and whenever she wasn't there I would climb up and slide down the pole. I presume it was my smile and faraway look that gave the game away. Eventually she told to stop using the frame altogether, but I was so addicted that I didn't stop. Finally, I was called to the headmistress's office and banned from using the climbing frame, without being given a reason. I can't remember when it dawned on me what had been happening, probably in the bath a few months later, but writing about it fifty-odd years later explains what a good but innocent feeling it was. If only it had stayed in my trousers a bit more often in later years... but more of that to come.

6

SECONDARY SCHOOL, SPORT, STUTTERS AND SECURITY

▼▼▼▼▼▼▼▼▼▼▼▼▼▼▼▼▼▼

And so to secondary school. Two years to go before teenager status, but my home life didn't change. Mixing with older and more street-wise children ensured I led a dual life. My home life was my secret. I preferred being at school to being at home, but when my mam needed me at home to help with my sister, brother and subsequent babies, go shopping or accompany her on a begging mission, I always had a handwritten note signed by her bearing a lie about some illness to explain my absence to the teachers.

I spent more and more weekends at my grandma's home. At school I threw myself into training for swimming, speed and life-saving and cross-country running. I'd found two sports I was particularly good at and it must have given me a release from the problems I had at home.

The drunkenness and beatings continued, however. There was one very nasty incident I witnessed when my 'dad' came back from the pub with his sister and her husband, a nice couple normally. They were all drunk. Not my mother though. She was heavily pregnant with my future sister and we had been reading together as usual waiting for him to come back from the pub. As soon as they came into the house he started shouting, building up a nasty attitude that we recognised all too well and which we knew would lead to her being beaten. I stood in the doorway with my books watching and waiting, but had some comfort with my uncle being there. My uncle, who was a lorry driver and much bigger than my dad, pulled him away from my mam. But when he released him my dad called my mam a whore and hit her with a massive swinging uppercut punch into her heavily pregnant stomach, then launched himself on top of her, trying to throttle her again.

My auntie started the screaming and ran out of the house shouting for help. My brother and sister were crying upstairs. I watched my uncle pull him off my mam again, and he started hitting my dad with his fists. That part was great to watch, but my mam was lying on her side being sick, and then the usual happened; the male neighbours men arrived, followed by their wives, followed by the police and then the ambulance. The only unusual thing that happened that night was my auntie attacking the police as they dragged my dad away.

They say bad things run in the family, and from secondary school I've always lived with the fear that a part of him will surface in me. Are these fears unfounded? I'm in my sixties now, and if I were to show any of his evil traits I'm sure they would have surfaced by now. But my memories of him and his behaviour are still so vivid that they haunt me. Will writing this book, certainly of my early life, not just be cathartic but help to remove some of the fears and demons I've retained?

I wasn't always feeling sorry for myself of course. I felt sorry for Albert in a big way once. I was at home helping my mother one day, instead of being at primary school, and we were listening to 'Lunch Box' or 'Workers' Playtime' on the radio. I listened to a story – I didn't know about monologues then – by a man called Stanley Holloway about a lion eating his son. When the animal keeper asked him if he was sure it was his son the lion had eaten, his dad said, 'Am I sure? There's his cap'. I couldn't accept that a father could be so flippant about his son being eaten by a lion and it really upset me for weeks. It must have been a relatively quiet time in our lives for me to feel more sorry for some other boy, rather than myself. Many, many years later I memorised the monologue 'The Lion and Albert', and on many occasions, to prove I don't stutter any more, I've recited it to friends and colleagues. Once I delivered it to hundreds from a stage on a large cruise liner.

I don't know how long my dad was in prison, or even if he was incarcerated there, but after my third sibling, my sister, was born I was taken by my mam to see him at a secure establishment which she described as a 'mental home', near Derby, about thirty miles and three bus rides away from our house. The many doors we had to go through were locked. He was definitely under lock and key, at last. When we arrived and walked past all the vacant staring, prisoners, residents or patients, we found him at a table making a wicker basket. For the first time in my life I saw him as a normal person. He was clean and smiled as he talked to my mam and showed her another half-dozen baskets he'd woven. He even asked me how I was doing at school and how my swimming was. I remember keeping my eyes down and not speaking to him, but making sly glances at the other inmates or patients working on their own crafts, or sitting smiling, staring off into space. There should have been some climbing frames for them. I hated being there, I hated being in his company and couldn't wait to leave.

They were holding hands at some point and I heard him saying the treatment was working and if he kept taking the tablets he would never drink again. Even though I was only a kid I couldn't accept he was going to change, and my opinion of him didn't waver. I hated him. Looking back I think my mam should have taken my next in-line sister for company, not me. I couldn't wait to leave him there and hoped he would never come back to us. I recognise now that even at that age my stubbornness had become deeply rooted and that I owe my inability to forgive easily to him.

I remember going there at least four or five times to visit him, so I couldn't have made a very good case for my mam to take my sister instead. I think she preferred me because we both read library books on the journeys. I think it's called escapism.

Of course he did come home eventually, but until then, home life was more than passable. There was no screaming or fighting, no nightmares, police or hospital visits. There was a male friend of my mam's who came and stayed for a few hours on a few nights during his absence, whom I recognised from earlier visits, presumably during my dad's other incarcerations. My mam's lovemaking shouts and cries always woke me and annoyed me. But those sounds, embarrassing as they were for a child to listen to, were better than cries for help. I was always her supporter, despite some nagging suspicions at times.

Finally come home he did, and we had at least a year of

him working, no drunkenness, and new clothes for me one Whitsuntide. We also had comics delivered, the *Dandy* for me and the *Bunty* for my sister. Happy days, but when the newsagent's bill wasn't or couldn't be paid the deliveries stopped. Still, it was a vintage year.

It was during this period of relatively normal family life that I experienced something which I thought at the time, and have thought many times since, made me different from my family and most of my friends. Behind my best friend's house were large empty fields and beyond them bluebell woods. One of my better-off gang mates had a tent and I was one of about eight invited to spend the night in it. It was in the middle of a field, close enough to hear the owls in the woods but only about three hundred yards in a direct line to our front door, obstructed by a line of houses and a road.

It was quite a walk down our street to get to the snicket gate to enter the fields. Of course it wasn't a problem at night, when the neighbours were in bed, to climb over their fences at the back of their houses and then up their garden path and out of the front gate into our street. This was common practice when we weren't camping, so long as were dressed as commandos, or at least wore balaclavas. It must have been in the summer holidays, because no one had blankets or sleeping bags, just our day clothes and a campfire just outside the tent door. It was great fun, especially when a couple of lads went home as it got dark, to our own imitation of owl hoots and laughter.

What sticks in my mind most, and what made me think I was a bit different from my family and peers, happened after I woke in the early hours and needed a drink. I walked back home in the dark for a drink of water and looked at the stars in amazement. There were millions in view and they seemed so close. The more I stared the more they made me feel really insignificant. For at least half an hour I stood drinking a cup of water on our path just staring at them and wondering where I fitted into this universe and what my life was about. It had a profound effect on me.

If we'd had a gate like everyone else in the street I'm sure there could have been a great photograph of me leaning on it, staring into space, holding a cup of water, an eleven-year-old hoping for a future. It was a common sight to see during the day, the hard-working men leaning on their gates, wearing grey, once white, singlet vests, heavy trousers with big belts and their braces hanging down, in slippers, holding large mugs of tea and talking to anyone walking past. Our gate had been used as firewood of course, along with the coal-house door, when we were short of coal, years ago. I still smile wistfully today, thinking of me as a kid, standing there with my enquiring look and holding my cup of water, alone and inquisitively staring at the stars.

Everyone was still asleep when I got back to the tent. When I started talking about what I'd seen and asking what it meant, none of the other kids were interested. Making the campfire and sitting round it toasting bread on long toasting forks was all that seemed to matter to them, and talking about the big animal noises that kept them awake all night.

Mind you, I almost didn't make the camping night out. It was only because the police didn't turn up that I was allowed to go. I was playing a game called 'stretch' with a lad from our street. This involved facing each other and throwing a sheath knife to the side of your opponent's foot. You start with your feet together. The knife had to stick in the ground and be no more than a foot away from your opponent's foot. You moved your foot to where the knife was in the ground, picked it up and did the same to your opponent. The one whose legs were so far apart that he couldn't stand up lost the game.

We'd played this a few times and I was good at throwing knives, or so I thought. I was stretching the game out a bit by getting the knife to stick in the ground closer to my mate's foot each throw when the inevitable happened. My last throw stuck in his foot. Off he went screaming for his mam, sounding more like a police siren than a kid in pain, the knife waving about as he ran but not falling out of his foot. I hid amongst the weeds until his mam came round shouting and between her and my Mam I was dragged round to their house to apologise to him. His sister was wrapping a bandage around his foot and he went off to the doctor's. Being old beyond my years I knew not to ask for my knife back. I was confined to the house as we waited for the police to arrive. It must have been too minor an event, compared with their usual reasons for attending at our house, so at the last minute I went camping.

It was about this time that a gang member and I went round dustbins collecting empty toothpaste tubes. We knew they had some lead in them, and as we were naturally adventurous and inventive, we melted them down in a crucible in my friend's garden, made the shape of an aeroplane in some sand and poured the molten whatever-it-was into the mould. After it had cooled we had our very own bomber. Even we knew that throwing something so heavy wouldn't be practical, so he fetched a chair from their house while I built a small pile of bricks and laid their long wooden clothes prop across it with one end of the ground. He stood on the chair and I placed our lead bomber plane on the other end. The intention was to see how high we could 'fly' it. As I backed away, after a couple of attempts to make it stay on, he jumped, the bomber flew upwards, and on its maiden and only flight one of the wings took a piece of flesh and bone from just above my left eye.

By the time I'd run home screaming for my mam, my front was covered in blood and my left eye resembled a cricket ball. No doctor's this time, it was straight into an ambulance to see if I'd lost my eye. I hadn't, but I still have a very noticeable scar to remind me of that escapade.

7

BOXING AND BURGLARY

▪▪▪▪▪▪▪▪▪▪▪▪▪▪▪▪▪▪

As I moved into my teens I joined the army cadets to learn how to box. Through constant running and swimming, I was fitter than anyone else I knew. That's where I channelled all my feelings and anxieties. It was always my intention to be able to sort my dad out physically as I grew older, and I dreamed of the day I could deal with him myself without the police being asked. I wonder how many kids go to sleep most nights dreaming of one day being able to beat their dad up.

I also wonder how many kids are woken up in the middle of the night by the sound of their dad, out of breath, carrying stolen food, alcohol and household goods upstairs after burgling the local shops. Or how many kids go down to light the fire before anyone else in the morning and see chicken feathers floating all round the house and smell the innards and carcasses in the bin, from the poultry stolen from the local farm.

I was horrified at what he was doing, no doubt selfishly because I didn't want to be further tainted by association, and told my mam I knew. Her response at these times was that we had to have food. Mine was to ask why he couldn't just go to work like my mates' dads. It was always stolen Lurpak butter on our table though, and not margarine. I have a penchant for fine food nowadays; perhaps I owe him a debt for that influence.

Although there was an improvement in my 'dad's' behaviour because the tablets he was taking made him physically sick when he drank alcohol, he would fall off the wagon on purpose by pretending to take them or lying about having taken them, and immediately revert to drunken wife-beating. At these times I used to help my mam by keeping him distracted as she opened his capsules and mixed the contents in his mashed potato or she kept him distracted and I did the deed. This wasn't always productive, because he would realise he'd mistakenly taken whatever drug it was when he threw up after his first pint in the pub. He'd then come back from the pub in a foul temper, punishing and beating her for embarrassing him in front of his mates.

It was always bad for my mam and throughout my life there I repeatedly asked her to leave him and divorce him.

One of his most memorable acts of abuse, as far as I was concerned, was after he'd beaten my mam to get the rent money and having been given it, got himself ready for the pub. He stood in front of the mirror, smiling at himself as he combed Brylcreem into his hair and put a jacket and tie on. He swaggered out of the house, one hand in his right trouser pocket. His exaggerated swaying made him look like a drunken sailor on the deck of a ship in a turbulent sea. I went upstairs and looked out of my bedroom window and saw him swagger across the road. My mam was still lying on the floor and sobbing. His swagger was so exaggerated that I hated him with every fibre of my being. Then, to rub salt in the wound, I watched as he walked up to a woman coming the opposite way, holding two small children by the hand. He stopped to talk to her, ruffled the children's hair, then took some money out of his pocket and gave them something each. I couldn't believe it. The woman was shaking her head to say no, but then as he walked off in the direction of the pub he turned and the two kids were waving at him and laughing. That was our rent money. I have never told my mam what I'd seen. I just let my hatred for him go deeper inside me.

In answer to the question you are probably thinking now, the answer is a resounding no. I have always had a safety valve that stops me drinking to excess – with the odd exception, but without consequence. I am not violent in drink, more inclined to be funny and fall asleep in the middle of a sentence. I do however, have a violent disorder – or so it's been called – when I'm faced with a woman who's been beaten by a man. Fortunately I have had a career that's enabled me to show a bit of violent disorder whenever I've arrested such men for assault, as I will tell you later.

8

COCK OF THE SCHOOL, AND A LIFESAVER

▪▪▪▪▪▪▪▪▪▪▪▪▪▪▪▪▪▪▪▪

At the age of 14 I joined the army cadets at their base in the Drill Hall in Clay Cross. It wasn't long before the trainer advised all and sundry that I was a future British champion in the making. I can't remember what division this would be in, but I was under ten stone and six feet tall with fast fists, a long reach, and built like a whippet with a terrier attitude. That was the trainer's description, not mine, but I liked it. The only problem was I didn't like hitting my opponents, preferring to dance around and shadow box like my hero at that time, Cassius Clay.

When I'd become quite proficient at this sport I remember saying to one opponent that he would never be able to hit me and would get too tired to lift his hands up eventually. Typical Cassius Clay style! In the third round neither of us landed a punch, in my case out of choice, until out of the blue he planted a hard glove on my nose, bursting it, blood everywhere, and I immediately turned into what the trainer wanted me to be. I chased the poor lad round the ring, over the ropes and out of the building before I calmed down and he got away. I resigned from the cadets because I didn't like what I saw in myself, and the other lad always avoided me despite me admitting it was my fault.

There was one good thing to come out of it though. I became, almost by default, Cock of my School. Most of the contenders pulled out once the schoolboys and girls formed a ring at the back of the fire station and I walked into it and took up my boxing pose. I understood from then on that confidently facing someone down, with a few choice words, would often win a fight before it started. I've used that technique many, many times as a police officer, in uniform, plain clothes or off duty, to get the desired result. It hasn't always worked, and I've had knife scars and other noticeable injuries, including being knocked unconscious, experiences which have been great talking points over the years.

I've mentioned that sport was my saving grace, but I know my ability to swim and life-save was the one and only reason I was accepted into the police as a Cadet.

Just after the Olympics in Tokyo in 1964, when Scotsman Bobby McGregor (Robert Bilsland McGregor) won silver in the 100 yards freestyle, or front crawl as we called it, I bettered his silver medal winning time over the first twenty-five yards. It was timed and recorded by my friendly PE and swimming teacher, Mr Briggs. He never told me at the time that I'd swum that fast, but the headmaster made an announcement at the following Friday morning assembly. He related my speed to that of my hero in Tokyo, which had created a new school record in the process, and I was asked to stand up and enjoy the applause. The downside to all that was my first true young love, Nancy, finished with me straight after the assembly for not telling her first. No one believed me when I said it was news to me too. My record lasted until my school was knocked down in the late 1990s and changed to office blocks, so it will remain the school record forever.

My swimming exploits were not without their ups and downs. When I was at infant school and aged about six, I learned how to jump off the top of the three diving boards at our 25-yard pool before I could swim. I used to splash around and enjoy myself with the other kids, but I was addicted to the excitement of watching other boys and men dive off the platforms. I could jump off the side of the pool but eventually I moved up platform by platform, always jumping so I came up near the side of the pool rail. I loved the thrill. I taught myself to swim this way mainly because I had no fear.

Well that's not quite true: I had a major fear when I started secondary school because my swimming trunks were of knitted wool, far too big, and hand-me-downs from a bygone age. They didn't really bother me because I wasn't materialistic, and I was only jumping into the pool at first. However, they bothered me when I was climbing out because they were so heavy with water that I had to hold them up with one hand and squeeze the water out while I was still in them, and they did cause me a problem when the other kids laughed when I started diving in for races against the other school house teams. Even though I used my school belt, elasticated with a clasp fastener and with the top of the trunks folded over it, they would still slide down more often than not. If you think of my waist being about 28 inches and the trunks made for a 34-inch waist the picture is better painted. At the start of a race I always dived with my left hand holding my trunks and my right arm straight forward. I was of course nicknamed 'Heil Hitler'. It worked, but sometimes after making a turn at one end of the pool I would push off, leaving my trunks behind and then having to rely on those at the poolside to point them out to me so I could retrieve them at the end of the race.

On one of my regular visits to my grandma's house I noticed a fantastic pair of trunks taking centre display in the window of the milliner's shop on the corner of her street. They were red with a black anchor on the front and a white draw string and were tight fitting, made of nylon probably. I asked how much they were. One pound seventeen shillings and six pence, the lady told me. It certainly wasn't the type of shop any of our family would use, and I think she recognised that. It was a fortune. But I was going to have them, so I asked the lady to keep them for me. The fact that they were always displayed in the window on my weekly visits to my grandma summed up her attitude towards me. It didn't stop me going in to ask her almost every week to save them for me until I'd saved enough paper round money to get them.

Christmas was approaching and I was saving every penny for presents. Every time I passed I was in a state of panic in case they'd been sold. I lived and breathed for them.

When I had the money I also had enough to buy my grandma what I thought was a nice Christmas present, and I was using that visit to deliver her present and buy the trunks. I'd bought six glass tumblers from Woolworths.

They were painted in multi colours, gay in the truest term, and, I thought, classy glasses. I had three in each hand well wrapped in Christmas paper, on the outside. Unfortunately I hadn't wrapped them individually and when I put them down on the wall next to the shop, so I could look at the trunks resplendent in the shop window and soon to be mine, I heard a sickening cracking noise. When I unwrapped the glasses only the top one from each three had survived; four down, two to go. I was faced with a dilemma. I loved my grandma more than the trunks, so I put a ten shilling note in the top glass and for the first time in years I started to cry. Grandma could see I'd been crying when I walked in and she forced me to tell her what had happened, presuming it would be something to do with my dad as usual. She unwrapped the two glasses, saw the ten shilling note and asked me what the money was for. When I told her what had happened, she asked me what I thought she would do with six glasses. She told me she could only drink out of one at a time anyway and I could use the other one. She gave me the money back and told me to get off and buy my swimming trunks. She obviously realised I'd been crying at my own loss and not hers. Bless her.

I was off like a shot, and shortly afterwards I was parading in her living room naked apart from the best pair of swimming trunks ever made. And from that moment on I was the envy of every swimmer at every competition, even county ones. I was always asked where I got them from and how much they were. In all my time swimming I never saw another pair like them. Bespoke, I think it's called.

Another memorable swimming memory, also with its ups and downs, also comes from my secondary school exploits. The changing cubicles for the men were down one side of the pool and the ladies' cubicles opposite. One step out of the cubicle and you were into the pool. They were made for up to two occupants, but we would get up to four in on school visits and there were standard off-white towels issued to everyone. Our group had a competition with the towels that involved closing your eyes, masturbating and then hanging your towel on your erect penis like a peg. The one who kept the towel on longest won. I came second every time and the winner was the same lad every time, and he was skinnier than me! We had different challengers every week, sometimes in the showers after PE, but he was unbeatable. The innocence of youth! I hope he's still around to read this and really hope he can still raise more than a smile at the memory.

It doesn't seem right not to have mentioned my dad's antics for a while, so my last swimming memory is dedicated to him. The one and only time he came swimming with me he shamed and embarrassed me. I could put up with him showing off to everyone doing swallow dives and somersaults off the top board. When the whistle went to end our session we were getting changed in our cubicle. I stood on the floor to dry and he stood on the bench, jumping up and down and waving his trunks at the women in the cubicles opposite. The last thing a lad wants to see is his dad behaving like that.

At this point one of the slats on the bench snapped and his leg slid through, making him disappear from their view and land on his bottom. As he extricated himself he was angry, probably from acute embarrassment, and swore loudly that he was going to sue the council. As I was always much older than my years I calmly told him the benches were for sitting on and they might charge him for the repair. He got changed quickly and left before I did. Even though we'd walked the two miles to the pool together, he wasn't around when I came out. Small mercies.

9

FIRST LOVE, AND ETERNAL SHAME

■■■■■■■■■■■■■■■■

I might have been our school's fastest swimmer, best cross-country runner, even representing our school in county championships, and had the best-looking girlfriend, Nancy, but I had no social skills or graces whatsoever. Nancy was beautiful, bright and far more worldly than me. She laughed a lot and talked about her mum and dad openly and with affection, so it was quite obvious she was part of a loving family. Her dad was one of the first to buy a new Mini, in 1964, and I was as excited as she was when she told our classmates they'd done 70 miles per hour in it. She lived in a different world from me and when I met her parents I could tell they didn't approve of me. When I called for her one day I overheard them talking to her about the reputation of my dad and his brothers. But they were kind to me because I was in puppy love with their daughter.

I have two memories which to this day cause me great embarrassment, even hot flushes. Nancy invited me to their house for Boxing Day tea. I was fourteen. The house was full of their relatives and most of them were playing cards. There was plenty of laughter and good humour and I was welcomed in, introduced and invited to play cards with the adults. Later in the evening my girlfriend presented me with a boxed shirt wrapped in Christmas paper. The shirt was long sleeved and cream and it was obvious to all that something was wrong, as I went bright red, left the table and went to the door to leave. I tried to give my girlfriend a pound note I'd brought with me in anticipation of her giving me a present, but also in hope that she wouldn't. I told her I'd tried to find a Christmas present for her but couldn't. It sounded really lame, but I'd only ever bought Christmas presents for my mother and grandma. I'd never had a birthday party, so I had never really experienced people buying me presents either.

Her mum came to the door and told me not to be silly and come back in. She told me I didn't have to give anything. I left anyway, with my shirt, unable to explain myself properly and thinking that would be the end of our relationship.

I tried to explain to her at school that I'd walked the shops in Clay Cross and Chesterfield for weeks before Christmas and couldn't find anything to buy for a girl, even though I had the money from my paper rounds. I just didn't know what to buy and I shouldn't have gone to her house on Boxing Day. It made me so miserable and disappointed with myself, but I just didn't have the experience, knowledge or wherewithal to know what to do. I should have asked my mam for help. I should have known better, I should have tried harder, but I didn't, to my eternal shame. And it still hurts, because she and her family were so nice to me.

Social graces were a long time coming; I learned them only after I left home to live in digs with landladies who insisted on teaching me manners, in the nicest possible way. One of my landladies, the one I had the most respect for, even gave me elocution lessons because, in her words, she thought she'd enjoy having a conversation with me but couldn't understand me. And we were both from Derbyshire.

My second personal error, again based on lack of social skills involving my girlfriend, came just after joining the regular police force in Derbyshire. Even though Nancy wasn't my girlfriend anymore, we were still distant friends, mainly on account of her being a nurse in New Zealand. But I'll deal with that later, if I have the courage to remind myself again of my lack of etiquette, manners and reciprocal love.

10

A JOB AT FIFTEEN

I was the only one from my class to leave school at the age of fifteen. I left on the Friday and started working at Markham and Company Steelworks in Chesterfield the following Monday, as an apprentice fitter, and how I hated it! Greasy overalls and heavy steel toe-capped boots in a noisy, dirty and cold factory. The other apprentices loved it and embraced it. I was respectful to everyone above me, but never grasped the concept of standing over a lathe watching it spin and smoke, or forever filing pieces of metal a fraction of an inch at a time to make something fit something I would never see. At least in the lunch breaks I experienced kicking a football with boots on rather than sandals. I was exhausted from boredom by the end of the first day.

After a couple of months I was asked by my Uncle Gordon, who had facilitated my acceptance into the firm, if

I was going to enter the company's annual swimming gala at the local baths in Chesterfield the following week. Apparently in those days the owners of firms such as this did arrange annual events to show their appreciation of the men who were making them rich – or to help the employees become a better team, I can't remember which it was...

Being a new employee I hadn't heard anything about it, but my uncle, knowing I was a swimmer, had asked his manager if I could participate. After confirmation that I could enter, he gave me a list of the events and asked me to tick the ones I wanted to take part in. I said I would enter them all, including 25 and 50 yard races in front crawl, breast stroke, backstroke and butterfly, plus neat diving from the side of the pool and from the springboard.

I came second in the 25-yard breast stroke and first in all of the others. I know some of my colleagues were happy for me, but a lot more thought I was showing off, particularly when one of the owners of the company presented me with the overall winner's silver trophy, which, with the plinth showing previous decades of winners, was as tall as a two-year old child. But I knew I had to leave.

Whilst at secondary school, I had unwittingly carried out a couple of merciful deeds that were to shape my future beyond all hope or expectation. Our local beat bobby, Constable Williamson, lived on the immediate outskirts of our estate and he knew me for all the wrong, but not serious, reasons. Mainly football and cricket in the street, recovering balls from unforgiving neighbours' gardens, climbing lampposts (not sliding down them) and other acrobatic behaviour, and generally creating an atmosphere around me likely to cause elderly men and women potential heart failure. He was always stern, and my mates and I are living testimony to the stories that a slap on the back of the head from a member of the local constabulary did more good than harm. But the important thing is that he got to know me as a decent lad, and not just as the kid responsible for dialing 999 for his assistance to save my mother's life on a regular basis.

Our local constable had a daughter about my age and I'd witnessed her running the gauntlet of abuse and stones hurled by youths on our estate on many occasions, just because she was a policeman's child and therefore, they thought, fair game. She was a grammar school girl of course, and I never saw her out with any friends where we lived.

I was never close enough, physically, to help her in her hour of need but I did speak to some of the thugs and told them to leave her alone. It didn't work straight away, but on one particular occasion I was walking towards her when she was under attack. I chased the lads off, threatening them, and then walked her home, taunted by the thugs from a distance. I decided then that I would sort these lads out and I got them one by one over a few days. In most cases my threats of violence were sufficient to take care of her well-being.

11

ESCAPE PLAN

■▪■▪■▪■▪■▪■▪■▪■▪■▪■▪■▪■

After less than three months of wearing greasy overalls and heavy boots and falling asleep on the bus to and from work, I formulated a plan. One night after work I washed and changed and called on Constable Williamson. His small office and public counter was attached to his house, oddly enough almost next door to the pub my dad habituated. The official door said it was closed, so I knocked on his home front door and luckily his daughter answered and invited me in. She immediately told her dad that I was the one who had looked after her. Her mum smiled and asked me to sit down and did I want a cup of tea? He didn't behave as graciously or even as welcomingly as I'd hoped. I believe he thought I'd called to ask his daughter out, and, knowing what he knew about my family, he would no doubt rather have had my head ringing than wedding bells.

I could see that her mum was pleased that I took my shoes off as soon as I went in. My balaclava was sticking out of my pocket. It was quite obvious that her husband didn't discuss his work with her, or I'm sure I would have been left outside under the porch. Once the tea formalities were over with and her mum had repeated her appreciation of my protection of their daughter, I got straight down to business. I'll never forget my prepared sentence: 'I want to be a police cadet sir, and I was wondering if you could tell me how to join'.

There was no laughter or spluttering of tea and Rich Tea biscuits heading my way, as I had dreaded. In fact he was very, very considerate (and no doubt relieved) and told me there were forms to fill in and references to get, exams and fitness tests to undergo. Then he asked me to come back and see him again in a week's time and he would see what he could do in the meantime. I walked home thinking, 'I'm going to be a Police Cadet'. And how many times during the rest of my life have I wanted to do something and just gone ahead and done it – many times in the face of many obstacles, but with a blinkered self-belief that what I want will just happen? They all stem from the certainty and euphoria I felt that evening.

I even enjoyed my next week at work, but I couldn't wait to go back to the police station. We sat in the local bobby's office this time and he had a pack of application forms for me to fill in and sign. To my eternal relief and gratitude he filled the forms in based on the answers I gave him, ensuring there were no spelling mistakes and forming well-constructed sentences. He never once mentioned my home life.

He asked me for the names of two referees. This was a problem. Eventually he said he would put himself down as one reference and I offered Neil's dad as the other. I remember he asked me a lot of questions about my swimming achievements and he smiled a lot when I listed them with my usual enthusiasm.

I was beginning to panic when a month went by and I hadn't heard anything, so I called to see my mentor and asked if he thought I'd been refused. He made a telephone call there and then and then told me I had been selected to go for an interview at the divisional headquarters in Matlock the following week. He said he would have the letter with the details sent to his police station, and I was to call round and pick it up in a couple of days.

12

THREE BUS RIDES TO HEAVEN

■.■.■.■.■.■.■.■.■.■.■.■.

Everything happened so fast from then on. I'm ashamed to say I went off sick the day of my interview because there was no time to get annual leave approved. I telephoned the factory office from a phone box in the bus station in Chesterfield, not far from the factory I was supposed to be at, and told the office I was sick. I hadn't told my mam what I was doing. I hadn't told anyone. It would never occur to my mam, or my dad obviously, that I'd taken a day off work. So long as the fire was made and I wasn't there when anyone got up, no one would be concerned.

I caught three buses to get to Matlock, and after asking the locals where the police station was, I arrived about three hours early. I informed a sergeant on the reception desk that I was there for the cadet interviews and was early. He told me to wait in the public reception, and I had my first taste of what happened on a daily basis at a busy police station. People were coming in to report things lost and found, things stolen, to say they wanted their houses looking after whilst on holiday. Others were complaining about their neighbours' dogs and children and noise, and there were criminals coming in on bail to sign registers to prove that they were still in the country. It was fascinating.

Then suddenly someone in uniform popped his head round the door and told me I was supposed to be upstairs with the other applicants. I thought I'd had an interesting but possibly a bad start to the proceedings as I followed the officer up two flights of stairs.

It didn't get much better when I joined the other five applicants, because the first thing the Inspector of cadets asked me was, where was my PE gear? I had the clothes I stood up in, and the letter in one hand. He told me this session was a fitness test and I would be doing fitness assessments and running. I said I would be OK in what I was in, but I took my Beatles jacket off and put it on the back of the chair.

It was at this point that it dawned on me that my stutter was an impediment, and it started to concern me a bit. I wasn't used to being in that kind of company and putting more than a couple of sentences together. I did cheer up a bit when I saw my opposition though. They were all well-spoken and confident but overweight – or at least well-fed, and not very competitive-looking. On the other hand, I was totally focused, hung on every word that was said and did everything at a hundred miles an hour. I won everything and hardly raised a sweat, fortunately.

The ordeal only lasted a couple of hours and I went home pleased with the results but a bit concerned about the impression I'd made before the fitness tests started. I consoled myself that I had been respectful, called everyone 'sir' and listened intently to every word said. They were going to write to us all and let us know if we had qualified for the next stage. One of the sirs asked me if I wanted them to send the letter to my local police station. I immediately agreed, knowing it would give me another reason to spend time with my new best friend, role model and mentor, and perhaps seek solace.

I didn't get any additional information from my local constable friend, other than to pick up my letter inviting me to the second and final interview. I read and re-read it to make sure I didn't have to take anything with me this time. It advised me the exam was based on general knowledge and would take a maximum of two hours. I didn't want to tempt fate, so I asked for a day of annual leave when I went back to work. When the lady in the office asked me what I wanted it for I mumbled something about a swimming competition and she wished me good luck and said she was sure I'd win it.

There were only two of us who had reached the final stage and as we sat in the waiting room I remember him asking me if I played golf. Me – play golf! He was a couple of years older than me and not my type, but I appreciated his manners and attempt at conversation. But golf – me! There was more chance of me becoming a police cadet, I thought.

The Chief Inspector of Cadets came into the room and introduced himself. He was ramrod straight, at least six feet five tall with a twirling Air Force pilot-type moustache, clipped voice and a double-barrelled name. I think his name was Hanson-Fenwick. Definitely Fenwick. The other lad stood up to greet him and shook hands. The only hand I'd ever shaken was my girlfriend's on a cold winter's night walk, so when he held his hand out to me he must have thought he was holding a lettuce leaf and my face must have given the game away. What was I doing there?

He told us we were going into separate rooms and there would be two exam papers to complete and to spend one hour on each. This was the end of the line for me, I thought. I was wishing I'd spent more time at school, or even stayed on, and I was even starting to blame my mam for these failings, until I realised it was my dad's fault I had had such a poor attendance record. This was going to be more embarrassing than having to stand up and say I was a free school meals kid every day.

I finished both papers, after a fashion, but I was convinced that only my name and date were correct. I was absolutely flummoxed. I didn't even understand some of the questions, let alone know the answers. I sat and waited dreaming of what might have been, seeing myself as a hero in uniform arresting thieves and burglars and patrolling the streets making people feel safe.

One hour later the Chief Inspector came into my room, sat down in front of me and said, 'So you're the swimmer?' He was smiling and looked so dashing, nothing like my local bobby, role model, mentor and friend. He must have talked for half an hour about life-saving techniques and what I would do in this or that water scenario. I relaxed and talked, or stuttered, my answers and advice to his questions, forgetting all about my mostly empty exam papers.

Then he brought me back to reality and asked if I'd finished the question and answer papers. I think he saw the fear and tears welling up and pulled them over to have a read of them. He put them back in front of me and walked behind me, telling me to pick my pen up. He told me that I was obviously very nervous and not thinking straight and that I knew far more than I'd done so far. He told me which question to go to, read it out aloud and told me I must know the answer to that. He then dictated what to write down. This went on for the best part of half an hour. He stopped a couple of times, picked the papers up, checked them and then said we were almost there. Eventually he told me to stand up and to shake hands properly this time. I did my best, and it did feel a bit more manly this time. Then he said those words which I will never forget as long as I live: 'Congratulations, you've just scraped through your exams.' He told me to go back to the waiting room.

He must have then gone to see the other applicant, because they came into the room together. He told us to have a coffee and he would be back shortly. The other lad told me the exam was easy and asked me if I'd done all right. I told him I wasn't sure. I almost called him sir, too, he had such a confident air about him.

My guardian angel and pilot-cum-Chief Inspector of Cadets came in with his sergeant and told us that we'd both done well and we would receive a letter informing us of their decision as to who had been successful. I was immediately back in the doldrums and was amazed that the other lad came over, shook my hand and wished me good luck. I would rather have had a fight there and then and winner take all. But he had good social grace, manners, etiquette and all the other dignified attributes I so obviously lacked. I knew these were the qualities I had to learn, but I would need a teacher first. I set off home grudgingly admiring my opponent, in awe of the Chief Inspector of Cadets and wondering what other job I could do that didn't involve greasy, smelly overalls and steel-toe-capped boots.

The return bus rides were interminably long and I had

plenty of time to reflect on recent events. I also thought about England winning the World Cup a few months earlier. If only I'd had some football boots, I could have been a professional footballer playing for Chesterfield Town. How many chances would I miss in life through having a dad like mine? However, despite him, or to spite him, I was never down for long.

13

LIFE-CHANGING DAY, OR APRIL FOOL?

▀▄▀▄▀▄▀▄▀▄▀▄▀▄▀▄▀▄▀▄▀▄▀

The letter came on Saturday 18th March 1967. The Top of the Pops number one at this time was Engelbert Humperdinck's 'Release Me'. How appropriate! Nervousness doesn't come into it. I wanted someone else to open it and tell me what it said, but of course no one knew what I'd been up to. I sat in front of the fire staring at the envelope, then walked around the settee, sat down again, stood up, paced around and sat down again. Then I heard someone coming downstairs, so I carefully opened the envelope.

The first thing I noticed was that it had been signed by my RAF pilot hero. Then to the top:

Dear Mr Clements
On behalf of the Chief Constable I am delighted to advise

you that your application to join Derbyshire Constabulary Cadet Force has been successful. May I take this opportunity to congratulate you. [Blah, blah, blah...] Please report to the Divisional Headquarters at Matlock at twelve noon on Monday 1st April. You have been allocated digs in Rowsley, where you will be obliged to remain for a minimum of six continuous weeks before taking your first home leave. Please bring sufficient clothing and toiletries.

That's as close as I can remember it now (which I guess is pretty close, since it was the letter that changed my life), and I read it, re-read it, read it again and again, put it in my trouser pocket, took it out and read it once again, never once thinking the first of April was Fool's Day.

My emotions were indescribable. Elated, frightened, disbelieving, proud, excited, and nervous. I looked around the room at the ash trays, fag ends on ledges, broken furniture, curtains with rings missing, torn wallpaper, the jungle outside the window, and I think my last emotion was sheer relief.

Then I thought about my mam and dad. I could hear them in the kitchen making a cup of tea, and I started to think about what I was going to say. At that very moment Neil's dad rescued me. I heard him come into the kitchen and tell them 'I've just got a letter from the police asking me to be a referee for your Nick to join Derbyshire Police Force. What's going on?'

The three of them came into the front room, Neil's dad waving the letter and stared at me holding mine. It was comical really. My stutter took over when I told them I was joining the Police Cadets on the first of April. The only people who could have been more disbelieving than myself were the three people staring at me.

I told them I was leaving home and would be living in digs near Matlock. If you think this was followed by hugs and cries of congratulations, you couldn't be further from the truth. My dad went back to the kitchen and Neil's dad went home. My mam asked me if it was true, even though it wasn't something you could make up. I showed her the letter and she asked me how it had happened. My emotions couldn't be dampened, but between the two of them they made a good effort to reduce my elation. To be honest I think my mam was in shock, but she went into the kitchen and joined my dad drinking tea, and smoking of course.

I'd seen my relatively new girlfriend walking past our front window a short time earlier, so I thought I'd catch her up and break the good news to her. There was no acknowledgement from my parents when I walked past them out of the house.

Perhaps their attitude was right, in view of our family background, and this was shortly to be reinforced by my girlfriend.

I ran and caught her up after a few hundred yards and we held hands and carried on walking down the street. I said I had some news for her and told her about the letter I'd just received. She stopped walking and stared at me. Tall, slim, blond hair, blue eyes, very good looking, she said, with a look of disgust on her face, 'You're going to be a f****** rozzer!' She snatched her hand out of mine and walked off, leaving me standing on the pavement. I looked around to see if there was anyone around, not because they might have witnessed me being dumped, but in the hope of seeing a friendly face who might be proud, or at least pleased, for me. I carried on walking to Clay Cross and caught a bus to my grandma's. No phones for us in those days. My grandma made up for the others, even though she just kept repeating, 'I can't believe it!' I spent the whole day and night and the next morning telling her everything that had happened, before going home to a silent dad and a more interested mam.

14

POLICE CADET

■▄■▄■▄■▄■▄■▄■▄■▄■▄■▄■▄■▄■

I called round to see my mentor and had a cup of tea with
him and his family, and although I can't remember how I
showed my gratitude I do remember that they shared my
excitement. I never did find out how instrumental he was
in my acceptance, but as the years passed and I grew in
confidence and knowledge, I saw that I owed it all to him,
because of what he must have said and written about me.
His daughter and my mam also played a massive, if
unwitting, part in encouraging me to be a champion for
frightened females. I suppose my own determination to
reach for the stars helped too.

Going to work the next morning and then to the office
in my break was a sweet moment. I didn't tell any of the
people I worked with except the lady in the office who'd said
she thought I'd win the swimming competition when I'd lied

to her. Then I found my uncle who'd got me the job in the first place and told him. He congratulated me, in a hesitant manner, and I had no doubt that I was well and truly on the other side now. Word soon got out, and I was told by a man in a suit that I could finish that day and would be paid until the end of the week. So, that was that. The massive swimming trophy, a reminder of my few months as an apprentice fitter, sat proudly on my grandma's sideboard dominating her front parlour, not that the room was ever used, but I knew it was there.

My toiletries on the day of my leaving consisted of a toothbrush, toothpaste and a comb. I didn't shave and men, or at least the ones I associated with, didn't use deodorant. I threw my balaclava away, since I was joining the police, not the SAS. My spare clothes, the ones I wasn't wearing, would easily have had room to get tangled in a small shopping bag.

Neil and his mother, who said she was 'chuffed to bits,' gave me an old suitcase to leave home with and off I went. I left my four siblings behind; Margaret aged twelve, Gary aged eight, Gaynor aged five and Lisa aged three, a three-bedroom council semi, my mam, Barbara, and the cause of it all, Stan. Neil, a year older than me, had just gone to university in Birmingham. First lad ever from our estate to go to university. No drama and no tears from me, just three bus rides to a new life – but with a gradual, growing apprehension and consternation about my stutter. Easy to write, but difficult to say! Happy? Ecstatic? Proud? Relieved? Yes please!

My first day was a blur. After arriving at the Divisional Police Headquarters in Matlock I was met by my guardian angel, the Chief of Police Cadets. It was very formal and short. No handshakes, just a quick word of welcome and the advice to be proud of my role in the police. I didn't need telling twice. No one could be prouder or more excited.

I was taken by police van to meet my landlady and family in Rowsley and to drop my suitcase off. Their house was an end-of-terrace, stone-built, double bay-windowed property straight out of a country house magazine, with a large back garden and garage in a picturesque little village with fantastic views up to the Derbyshire Dales. I was introduced to my own bed in my own bedroom with a wardrobe and bedside table with a reading light – and not a fag end in sight! How could this be happening to me?

My Irish landlady and landlord, Mr and Mrs Drabble, were softly spoken and their infant son and dog were playful. I never did get to call them by their first names, and at first it was more like M'lord and M'lady.

As I left the house to go back to the police station, M'lady told me dinner would be at six o' clock. As I left with the constable assigned to me on my first day, I was already looking forward to coming back.

The most exciting part of the day was to find and spend time in the force's uniform clothing lorry. I was the only cadet in a line of constables and sergeants queuing for replacement uniforms. When it was my turn I was measured and given piles of clothing, including serge trousers, tunics, a cap with a blue band around it and half a dozen blue shirts with plenty of separate collars and studs, epaulettes and black ties. The most memorable moment was the word and number 'Cadet 8' being fixed to the epaulettes and tunics. I had become Cadet 8 Clements! This is me we're talking about here. I was bursting with pride and enthusiasm and trembling at the thought of walking into the police station at Matlock wearing my uniform. There was a bit of a hiccup though, in that my shoes were green suede and I was told I needed to purchase my own boots before I could wear my uniform.

When we reached Matlock I asked the constable where I could buy boots and he dropped me off outside a shoe shop he recommended. Thanks goodness my thoughtful grandma had given me ten pounds to tide me over until I got paid. Suddenly I was ready to go, but then there was the interminably long-drawn-out process of form filling in for the rest of the day. All I wanted was to put my uniform on. I was shown around the police station and told to come back the next day in my civvies again to finish off the formalities. My disappointment lasted only minutes, because then my RAF pilot lookalike, in shining blue serge uniform and white shirt, walked into the room, causing everyone around me to stand and those with hats or helmets on salute him. He told me he wanted to see me at nine o'clock the next day to talk about life saving.

15

MY OWN BEDROOM, AND NO ASHTRAYS

▪▪▪▪▪▪▪▪▪▪▪▪▪▪▪

I was taken to my new home by the constable in the police van, and I filled my wardrobe with my pride and joy. I tried every item on and practised tying a good knot. It was my first tie since my school tie, although I had bought a bright green cravat once, but just as they were going out of fashion, unfortunately. I was six feet tall and a wiry nine and a half stone. I thought I looked the part and the mirror confirmed my opinion. I was more like six foot three with the black shiny boots and peaked flat cap. I was ready to take on the world in terms of my clothing — but alas not verbally, yet.

My first meal was extraordinary. I was called to come down from my bedroom. This would always be the case. If I was in their house, I was in my bedroom or downstairs at meal times. Throughout my stay with them, I always

73

believed I couldn't intrude into their personal space. Their hospitality, my bedroom and the food were more than sufficient. My first meal started with soup, followed by a full chicken dinner, followed by jam roly-poly and custard — no feathers floating around the house — and we all sat at the dinner table. It wasn't Sunday and there was no sign of a celebration, just a glimpse of what heaven must be like.

After dinner I asked if I could take their dog for a walk. The back of their house looked up to the hills of the Derbyshire Dales, with only fields and trees separating the start of the hills and their garden. I walked their terrier for a couple of hours, getting to know the village, its back streets and footpaths up to the foot of the Derbyshire Dales hills. I had no idea that doing this on my first evening would be the beginning of stutter prevention.

And so to bed. To my own clean-sheeted, sweet-smelling bed, in a beautiful house occupied by a loving couple. How many miles – or lifetimes – was this from Clay Cross? Nothing could spoil this, could it? I knew there and then I would fight tooth and nail, anything and anyone, to stop anyone who tried to take this from me.

Breakfast was always cereal or porridge, followed by as many slices of uncut toast and jam as I could eat. And if that wasn't something to beat, I was given a small bag of sandwiches and fruit, every day, to take to work. This would be referred to as 'snap' in Clay Cross. It was called a 'packed lunch' here, just a few miles away. I was collected and transported by my police colleague for the final time, that first morning, back to Matlock Divisional Headquarters police station. This was my place of work and where my new life was to begin.

There was more form filling to be done, escorted tours and introductions made. There were no handshakes though, as I soon realised that despite my own pride, I was the lowest of the low in terms of rank and importance and if the truth be known, a bit of a dogsbody. But nothing could wipe the smile off my face and I was eager to learn everyone's rank, or civilian title and surname. My failsafe was to call everyone 'sir' to start with, apart from two other police cadets who were based in the station. They didn't speak to me that day, which was a bit disappointing, but I could see they were very busy filing, answering the phones and speaking to members of the public at the counter. How would I learn to do all that?

The answer came later that day, when I was shown into the grand office of the Chief Inspector of Cadets, my hero. He was quite official and told me that I would commence my cadet training the following day. I should report to Matlock police station at 9am the next morning, for the rest of this and the next week, for cadet training in the class room. I asked if I could wear my uniform and was told that in fact I must wear it and that my boots must be highly polished and my uniform pressed. I was told I must look smart at all times and represent my police station in the proper manner.

Could things get any more exciting? Yes they could. He asked me if I'd seen the open-air swimming pool round the corner yet. No I hadn't. My previous visits to our police station had been direct from the bus station and back again. I didn't know about Matlock, or its swimming baths, or its beautiful parks and the fast-flowing river Derwent running through it. But I would soon. I could hardly wait.

It was also explained at this time that although I had been accepted as a police cadet in Derbyshire Constabulary, our force was being amalgamated with Derby Borough Police the following month and I was lucky to have joined when I did, as Derby Borough did not have a cadet policy. I was the last police cadet to be recruited by my employers. Lucky? Derbyshire Constabulary consisted of divisions, including Ashbourne, Bakewell, Belper, Chesterfield, Derby, Glossop, Melbourne and of course, the HQ in Matlock. Our new force would be called Derby County and Borough Constabulary. The county's rose and stag's heads emblems would be joined by the Derby Ram. The new force's Latin motto *vis unita fortior*, meaning 'strength united is greater', meant little to me. I was just overjoyed to be part of it. By the time I'd received a pay packet I would have been a member of two police forces. How's that for progress!

My third day as a police cadet, and my first in uniform, meant being on show to the public. I walked around the bedroom, then the house and then the garden to get some practice in. Mrs Drabble told me I shouldn't wear my cap at the table. Even though the bus journey was twenty minutes, I went to catch the eight o'clock bus and was even early for that.

I had no sooner reached the bus stop when a Rolls Royce stopped and the driver called me over. Should I ignore him or just tell him it was my first week as a police cadet and I didn't know anything? He was smiling as I bent down to his passenger window and after I replied that yes, I was going into Matlock, he told me to jump in and he would drop me off at the police station. If they — if anyone — could see me now! Whenever I was at the bus stop and he was passing he would always stop and give me a lift. Heaven would not have to wait; I was already there.

I'd walked 100 yards from my digs to the bus stop and another 100 yards to the police station from the Rolls Royce, and I still smile at how loudly and ferociously my heart was beating against my rib cage. It was a relief to get into the police station without further incident, but the excitement and adrenaline it brought was addictive.

The cadet training included some worldly-wise cadets from outlying police stations who'd been through their initial training at our headquarters and had been allocated sub-divisional police stations where they were more hands on. 'Hands on' included sometimes being left in charge of the police station if the station sergeant had been called out to help in a local incident, or if he was in the local betting office, one superior cadet told me. My target, I was told, was to catch up with the others, as I was the last cadet to join our constabulary, and there wouldn't be any more.

The first thing I had to arrange was to open a bank account in Matlock. I chose National Westminster. A lot of the training over the next week and a half was about behaviour and responsibility and understanding what was needed to become a real policeman. We were to constantly learn and practise what is needed to become a real policeman. There was very little about the law itself. I was taught at the beginning how to salute; a very British, stiff upper lip and energetic type of salute, showing absolute respect. Not like today's meaningless efforts seen on TV. Practise at home in front of the mirror, I was told, and woe betide you if you were ever disrespectful to a senior officer.

We were taught to recite the prefix to witness and suspect statements, including, 'I make this statement of my own free will, etc.' (offender) and, 'This statement is true to the best of my knowledge and belief etc' (witness). We were taught how to write reports that always commenced with 'To the Chief Constable' regardless of which senior officer it was being sent to and always ended with, 'I remain, Sir, your humble servant, Cadet 8 Clements'. Discipline, that's what it was, and a daily reminder of where you were in the strict hierarchy of a public institution.

At our first lunch break all the dozen or so cadets put

civilian jackets over their police shirts and went into Matlock, to walk or shop or eat. All but one, that is. I wasn't allowed out, having only my uniform to wear, on my own. I had to be accompanied by a real policeman if I wanted to walk around the town centre, at this stage of my career. I didn't mention I had travelled to work that day with my uniform proudly on display. It didn't stop me from wearing it to and from work either in the early days, especially when I discovered I was allowed to use the local buses free of charge. I hadn't joined the police to hide my vocation.

16

T-T-T-TRAGEDY!

■.■.■.■.■.■.■.■.■.■.■.■.■.■.

I ate my sandwiches with another cadet and was introduced to another sport I would become good at – snooker. He took me to the fourth floor, showed me the two snooker tables and taught me how to play, or at least the basics on that first visit. I became quite proficient over the coming months. Many times I would work on the ground floor office facing the public, answering phones, including handling the switchboard or filing reports and dealing with incoming mail, and I would often miss my allocated lunch break. Many times I would miss it entirely, but sometimes a sergeant or older constable would tell me to take a break and at these times the snooker tables were not in use. I would practise on my own for a half hour, or even stay after my shift to practise.

Most of my duties at this stage didn't demand much in

the way of eloquence from me, so it was not until my second week of training that I discovered to my horror that my stutter might be the undoing of me. We were being taught how to give evidence on oath in a pretend courtroom, and the seriousness of giving evidence was explained in some detail. Perjury meant a prison sentence for a police officer, so accurate and considered verbal statements were a priority whenever we were in the witness box.

When it was my turn to take the Holy Bible in my right hand and repeat what the Court Usher would say, panic took over. We would start by giving our name and rank followed by the words, 'I swear by almighty God, that the evidence I shall give, shall be the truth, the whole truth and nothing but the truth.' Easy to write and easy to remember. 'Nicholas' wasn't too hard. 'Clements' could be a problem sometimes. But 'God' was nearly impossible and only arrived after gurgling sounds, splutters and bulging eyes, followed by a mini explosion of His name. My shouting of 'God' sounded more like blasphemy and was usually accompanied by a release of nervous laughter from my peers. This would immediately be followed by shouts from the training sergeant to behave.

There was no doubt in my mind that I had to overcome this disability before my reputation was in tatters, along with my career. This was a serious issue and an obstacle I had to overcome, particularly as it was less than a couple of weeks into being a cadet. Most conversations with me began with a piss take - 'Hello N-N-N-N-N-N-Nick,' stuttered and spluttered by laughing fellow cadets and some other staff. Cruel, though obviously funny for those taking the mick, but it was nothing compared to what I would face in the line of duty as the years progressed – when I didn't even have a stutter.

My first weekend arrived and I was reminded that I
could not go home for the first six weeks, so I was confined
to the bedroom in my digs or if I was outside, I would walk
the dog, or swim in the outdoor pool in Matlock. My meals
were included in the monthly payments made by the force
admin and my landlady was paid a bit more for the first six
weeks to include the weekends. These payments were made
from my salary before I was paid. I seem to recollect that
my monthly salary was £52 and some shillings, but after my
lodgings were deducted I had about three pounds a week to
spend. I paid my grandma back the ten pounds she had
loaned me on my first visit home, but we had an
understanding over the subsequent months that I could
borrow it again, and again, a fortnight after being paid.

Before I left the police station on the Friday evening I picked
up a pile of *Police Review* magazines and some copies of
Police Gazette, which reported on current crime and wanted
persons. I thought they would make good reading over the
weekend and give me a better understanding of my future
requirements. I started reading one of the *Police Review*
magazines on the bus and at the same time had what can
only be described as an epiphany – a vision about how to
stop my stuttering. Straight after tea, I took the terrier and
the *Police Review* up the footpaths towards the hills and
dales. As soon as I was out of earshot of the houses I started
to read the magazine. Silent reading doesn't involve a
stutter, so I started reading quietly at first, and then started
raising my voice until I could be heard at least a hundred
yards away. I read a paragraph or two out loud, then chose
one that was worthy of remembering and kept repeating it,
memorising it until I could repeat it without looking at the
page. I did this for a couple of hours and came back to my

digs with a sense of self-belief that I might eventually control my stutter.

My first Saturday away from home, or rather from my grandma's, I had a choice of repeating my reading out loud whilst walking or visiting Matlock swimming baths. I chose to walk and read, and spent all day in the Derbyshire Dales with the terrier, talking to myself in a loud voice. I also saw the double benefit of learning and improving my stutter at the same time. Swimming the next day was followed by more walking and talking, and my first weekend away was over before I knew it. I must say that my stutter didn't improve as dramatically as I wanted it to, but practice makes perfect. As the nights got lighter, the more time I spent practising. I did attract attention and got some weird looks from ramblers on occasions. I was so immersed in my self-help that I was upon them before I'd seen them. But other than that, there were no yellow vans coming to take me away, or suspicious police officers spying on me.

After my first two weeks of cadet training I was feeling much more comfortable in my surroundings and with the police officers, civilians and the two other cadets in the station. I shadowed the most senior cadet and it wasn't long before I was enjoying doing bits on my own, particularly as I started early and stayed on after my shifts had finished. My mentor played snooker and we spent our breaks playing, and if he wasn't available other staff would suggest a game with me if they saw me practising on my own. Within a month I was speaking to members of the public, answering phones and operating the switchboard, and constables and admin staff were calling me Nick. Sergeants and above always referred to me as Cadet 8.

At about this time Mrs Drabble told me that as I was with them for six continuous weeks, she would do my washing, rather than me having to take six weeks' worth to my grandma's. Mrs Drabble had already taught me how to iron my trousers and the sleeves of my tunic and get the creases out of my new shirts. I gave her the carrier bag of dirty washing and she asked where the rest was. I was nonplussed, but not embarrassed. There were two pairs of underpants, my long-sleeved cream shirt from Nancy and one police shirt, plus a couple of collars. When I told her that was all there was, she told me in future I was to change my underpants every day and my socks and shirt twice a week. I had plenty of police shirts, but I had to leave the police station at lunchtime the next day to buy more underpants. She was quite nice about it but very firm, and wanted to see what I had bought. I had been brought up to have a weekly bath on Sundays and change my clothes at the same time. I agreed willingly that this kind of living and learning was progress and I was pleased and proud to be changing this way.

17

TOILET ETIQUETTE

■▪▪▪▪▪▪▪▪▪▪▪▪▪▪▪▪■

I did have a few very embarrassing moments though, at work and in my digs. I didn't consider the underpants issue one of them. The most embarrassing happened one Sunday evening about a month into my new job. The family was at church and I was in my bedroom reading police books as usual, but desperate to use the toilet. Up until now I'd only used it for a wee. I always managed to use the toilets at work for a poo and the swimming baths for a shower. I contemplated getting a bus into Matlock, but the buses didn't run that often on a Sunday. I considered the bathroom to be theirs and a rather private room, so the less time I spent in it the more comfortable I felt. But they were at church and I could open the window to let any smell escape and I would make sure it was just as spick and span afterwards. Fatefully, I made the wrong decision. The embarrassment makes me wince even now.

I'd obviously waited too long and had become constipated. When it did finally arrive it was like a mini-telegraph pole, at least two thirds of it sticking out above the water line. That was my view of it for the next twenty minutes or so as I flushed, waited, flushed and waited some more. In desperation I went to the kitchen and boiled the kettle. I thought boiling water would help soften it, break it down and flush away. Each time I returned upstairs with a full kettle of boiling water the smell was worse and only the pole above the water line was breaking up. It would not flush away, and I was regretting my decision to use their loo. 'Regretting' is too mild a word. I was sweating with fear, and panicking. I used my towel to waft the smell towards the open window, but I knew from my visits to the kitchen that the house had been overtaken by the smell.

We have toilet brushes now, but I don't think they'd been invented then, or at least I'd never seen one and Mrs Drabble didn't have one. In desperation I ran outside and pulled a stick out of the garden which was holding a plant or something up, ran back in and started to push the offending blockage down the toilet at the same time as flushing it. It eventually worked and I used half a toilet roll wiping the bowl and the splashes from the rim and floor. I was beside myself with fear that they would return whilst the smell was still there.

Just as my heart was starting to slow down a bit, I heard their car turning into the drive. I threw the smelly stick out of the window into the garden just as the car stopped nearby. I ran downstairs, picked up the dog lead with one hand and the dog with the other and met them on the drive and told them I was going for a walk. Nothing unusual in that of course. As they entered the house I picked the offending stick up and headed for the hills as dusk was starting to settle. I threw the stick under some bushes a few hundred yards away and kept walking.

When I returned, hours later, I could see from a distance that all the windows were open. My embarrassment was acute. I hung the dog lead up, said goodnight and went straight to my room. The next morning I woke early enough to walk to work missing out on breakfast. I went back to only using their toilet for a wee and a wash for the remainder of my stay there. The couple of times I was desperate during my remaining weekends there, I took the dog for a walk with toilet paper stuffed in my pockets, and used a hedge bottom a couple of miles away from civilisation.

Mrs Drabble never spoke about the incident, but that might have had something to do with the shameful look I had for days afterwards and her good grace, manners and consideration. It was the learning curve I was on and I never looked backwards — only to my future, or that's how my life seemed to be, without any particular planning on my part. I decided never to be constipated again.

This is not something one should be discussing, and of course I've never mentioned it verbally to anyone since. But I was still only sixteen coming up to seventeen years old, a non-smoking, non-drinking virgin with stars in my eyes, determined to overcome every obstacle put in my way and become a successful police cadet. I wanted to be someone at least my grandma would be proud of in the first instance. That's a bit unfair, because later on she told me my mam was proud of what I'd achieved, although my ears never heard that.

I did learn a very valuable lesson from this bathroom incident and I've tried to remember to use it all my life; if you know something you are about to do might cause someone acute embarrassment, just don't do it. Unless, of course, the recipient is a nasty, evil, drunken wife beater. Thank you, Mrs Drabble, I learned a lot from you and because of my improved self-awareness and consideration you've helped a lot of other people out too. And of course, reporting my nightmares at about this time to a senior Police Officer was a life changer too. So I would say again, thank you m'lady. My wonderful life had been blighted, in the short term to say the least, by my post mortem experience. Nevertheless I know I came back stronger and more determined, if sadly no wiser.

18

SNOOKER, AND POTTING THE PINK

■▼■▼■▼■▼■▼■▼■▼■▼■▼■▼■

Another incident while I was new into my cadetship, but post the post mortem incident, did help my progress in relationship building, but was by no means planned. As I've said, I would play snooker at odd times long after official meal breaks were over. On this occasion I decided to practise my snooker skills for half an hour and went to the top floor games room. I opened the door to be confronted by a woman's face, obviously in ecstasy, leaning over the shoulder of a man whose back was towards me. His serge trousers were round his ankles and her ankles were wrapped around his waist, her knickers on her left ankle. Her bottom was perched on the edge of the snooker table.

We had obviously all arrived at the same time, so I

didn't spoil their ultimate enjoyment. I particularly admired his response when he realised I was standing there, wide-eyed and open-mouthed. 'Cadet 8, wait outside!' She was still smiling, but wickedly, with her naked legs still wrapped around his waist. He was the Admin Sergeant and she was one his civilian employees. I'd only seen my sister naked, and never a naked adult – a live one anyway. Although this woman wasn't fully naked, it did amount to a very sexual vision, and the fact that she was smiling at me when he was shouting at me added to my excitement. I rapidly left the room, but instead of waiting outside I rushed downstairs, ran past my office area to the basement toilets, and whilst the image was fresh in my mind I relieved myself with great gusto.

I avoided the games room for a few days and was always respectful when in the presence of the Admin Sergeant lothario, whom I knew to be married, or the administrator, who wasn't married, by avoiding eye contact. I never mentioned what I'd seen to anyone and was rewarded a couple of weeks later when the lothario came into the games room as I was practising my snooker. He suggested we play a game together, and of course I agreed. There was no conversation to start with, but when he lined a ball up to play into the pocket his mistress's bottom had been perched over, he spent a long time looking at it before lifting his head up and smiling at me.

We played for a few more minutes before he said he had to go. He shook my hand and said 'Thanks'. I don't believe it was a thanks for the game either. After that both of them spoke to me in passing without any averted eyes. I was looking forward to losing my virginity even more, and if she'd invited me for a game of snooker I wouldn't have needed a cue, but dream as I might, that would never happen. Losing my virginity was still a long way off, unfortunately.

When I had done my six weeks' continuous service I was told to go home for a week. Half of me wanted to go home in the hope that I would be questioned excitedly by my family and friends about my new life. I was enjoying my life so much, but I was also sure my landlady and her family were looking forward to a having a break from me, so with some trepidation I went home. Knowing that I would be staying with my grandma helped. I'd written a couple of letters to my mam and grandma during the six weeks I'd been away so I hadn't lost complete contact during this time. But in any case it turned out to be a great break, spending time with my three sisters and brother, even though my excitement and my stories held no resonance for them. I had quality time with my grandma, who did appreciate my stories, even though she was understandably bewildered. I remembered to give her the ten pounds I owed her and she said she would put it in the larder and leave it there until I wanted to borrow again. How wise was my grandma?

She told me she couldn't wait to show me a letter she'd received from my old PE and swimming instructor at school, Mr Briggs. It was addressed to her, not my mother, and it was about me. She was beaming at me as I read it, especially the part where he said that he and everyone who knew me should be very proud of what I had achieved and that he believed I had it in me to be a leader of men one day. Imagine that, from a schoolteacher!

That week at going-home time I went to visit him at my old school. I waited for him outside the staff room, and when he saw me he asked me to join him in the room and we had a cup of tea together. He asked me a lot of questions about my career, as we both called it, and showed a genuine interest. He told me he'd started an evening gymnastics class and asked me to join. When I told him it was three bus rides from my digs to get to the school and I wouldn't get there in time, he simply said 'Get a moped or a scooter then'. The very next day I applied for a provisional motorbike licence, using my grandma's home as my address.

Before I knew it I was back at my digs, wearing my uniform proudly and doing my dog walking and talking in the hills in a loud voice every evening. I was learning loads about general policing and the criminal law and gaining personal confidence. My stutter now only reared its ugly head when I was under pressure, especially when some of the sergeants and inspectors fired questions at me and wanted immediate answers and, of course, when we practised giving evidence during my classroom training. I loved my life. I was making progress and I was really pleased with myself. I was permanently enthusiastic, excitedly happy and growing in confidence, if still a bit reserved in conversation.

Within a month my life could not have been better. I wouldn't have swapped places with the Chief Constable himself. It was summer and I was swimming at every lunch break. The manager said he liked to see me walking into the building in my uniform, as it was good for security. He also let me in for free, which encouraged more visits from me and saved me a fortune. His staff and a lot of other people commented on my swimming ability, knew my name and gave me a lot of confidence – something that had been, hitherto, sadly missing. My classroom training was a joy and I loved learning about what makes a good police officer and even learning some definitions of criminal law.

19

EXAM FAILURE – CAREER SUCCESS

The only interruption of my renewed joy and job satisfaction was when I was told, at one week's notice, that I had to visit a college in Derby and sit my O Levels in English and Maths, over a two-day period. I hadn't learnt anything more about these subjects since leaving school and again I looked back in anger at the number of schooldays I'd missed. When I took them this time, I just knew I'd failed when I walked out after each exam sitting, although not officially. I was back at work, a bit morose, but determined to read as much as I could about police work, past case histories, the law and topics in the *Police Review*, so as to prove I could one day be a police officer without educational qualifications. I didn't pass those exams, and I still haven't got a single educational certificate to my name.

But then an incredible thing happened. Within a couple

of weeks of miserably walking out of the college in Derby, the man I saluted most fervently, white charger or not, my Chief Inspector of Cadets, phoned downstairs and asked me to come and see him. I know from my classroom colleagues that all the cadets were fearful of him, but I adored him, in a very respectful way. I knew it would be to tell me I'd failed in my exams, again, but I had no hesitation and felt no trepidation in going to see him. No one wants to hear bad news, but if I was going to hear some, I would want to hear it direct from him.

After probably my best-ever salute, he made another memorable statement: 'Relax Cadet 8, you're not getting sacked, in fact quite the opposite. I'm very pleased with your progress. You've passed your probationary period. Congratulations.'

I tried to tell him I'd failed the exams I'd just taken, as it dawned on me what he'd just told me. I was still trying to give him reasons why he should sack me when he interrupted me sharply and dismissed me – from his office. Then he called me back from the doorway and reminded me that I should salute when dismissed, as well as on arrival. I was mumbling a constant stream of 'Thank you sir' and 'I'll never let you down, sir' and my salute must have looked as if it had been made by a clown.

I closed his door and leaned against it. His secretary asked if I was okay. Was I okay? In less than five minutes I'd told everyone in the police station my news, except those in the CID department. They were in a league of their own and not even to be smiled at by the likes of me, but nothing could get in the way of my joy and happiness. I would be a police constable in less than two years' time!

Although my relief was palpable, and brightly coloured my imagination in the most wonderful way, my life carried on the same. I was an avid reader of everything 'police', swimming four or five times a week and trying to pot as many balls in that famous pocket as possible.

I was also to be seen riding flat out on my newly-acquired moped – 30 mph on the flat – to get to my new love of gymnastics at night classes once a week at my old school, taught by another hero of mine. I could do somersaults and back springs on the floor, a very good impression of the Maltese Cross, and a somersault to finish off on the rings. I didn't have much muscle. The best description of myself at this time would be a super-fit, lean and wiry, non-drinking, non-smoking, naive virgin, coming to the end of his 16th year.

20

1967 – BELPER, AND MY NEW SAVIOUR

All good things must come to an end, or at least a change of direction must happen. I was called up to see my favourite Chief Inspector. My salute was as sharp as my increased confidence. I'd already been told by one of the office sergeants some months earlier that

I had failed my English and Maths 'O' Levels, so I wasn't expecting bad news – unless it was that I had to retake them. I was knocked back initially though, when he told me he was transferring me to the Sub Divisional Police Station at Belper. I knew of it, if not where it was. It was in fact twenty-five miles from Matlock and the same distance from my grandma's, but, significantly, as I was about to find out, only ten miles from Derby. I'd already upgraded my ancient moped to a red BSA Bantam 125cc, so travelling was more of a pleasure, or at least a bit faster, and I'd also learned how to change plugs and points.

As soon as I'd bought my second-hand Bantam I applied to take my test, and once again my intuitive nature helped me. I took the verbal instructions from the assessor to take the lefts, rights and left turns around the market area of Chesterfield town centre. These instructions were designed to allow the assessor to move from one corner to another in a tight area to watch my hand signals and manoeuvres from a distance. I was so busy watching out for him I almost crashed into a car at one of the junctions and my bike slid across the road with me under it, even though I was only doing about ten or fifteen miles an hour. The car driver jumped out and was in the process of asking me if I was hurt as I looked down the side road to see if I could see the assessor. I couldn't see him, so I jumped up and set off again as fast I could to get to where I was supposed to be. I did see him on a number of occasions, including the one where he jumped out in front of me holding his clip-board up and shouting at me to STOP! I was wincing with pain, but hoping against hope that he hadn't seen me sliding across the road. When I'd finished and eventually pulled up by the side of the assessor, outside the Test Centre, I made sure he couldn't see the torn clothes and blood down my left-hand side.

I'd passed the theory test with one hundred percent and now had my damaged fingers crossed that he hadn't seen my fall. He hadn't. I passed, and he helped me celebrate by taking the learner plate off the back mudguard. I literally scraped a pass!

But back to the person responsible for enabling my employment as a police cadet, who was now transferring me away from what was quickly becoming my comfort zone. My

Chief Inspector of Cadets quickly put my mind at rest when he explained that the Chief Constable was now very keen to start a police cadet swimming and life-saving team, to compete in national events. He told me that as the sergeant who had been given responsibility for setting it all up was based at Derby, Belper police station was a convenient place for me to assist him. If I'd been in the SAS I think it would have been called a field promotion. I always knew in the back of my mind that the reason my application to join the police cadets had been successful had been my swimming abilities. Fairly obvious really. This was the first time it had been mentioned in any official capacity though.

I left his office with a mixture of excitement and regret. I would be doing something I was very good at, within my role as a police cadet, but I would be leaving behind a life that was just about perfect. Perfect digs, to start with. I'd sampled the good life there. I'd had a couple of (platonic) girlfriends whom I'd met through swimming. Pubs were still a no-go, of course, and beer didn't appeal to me in the slightest, so my opportunities to meet the fairer sex and realise an ambition regarding my virginity were a bit limited. I knew I looked the part, tall and smart in uniform and fit and lean in my red swimming trunks with the black anchor. But my Clay Cross accent, coupled with my stutter, prohibited serious progress in that direction.

I made my farewells, but it was all low-key. The more I got used to the idea, the more excited I became. It was a new phase and hopefully more progress on the learning curve. It became a tremendous learning curve, in fact, and no doubt the most important phase of my life.

I went to my grandma's for the weekend with my now full to capacity suitcase strapped to the pillion seat behind me. Of course it was nine-tenths uniform, as I had little need for civvy clothes. I drove out over the weekend to reconnoitre my new police station in Belper. It was a converted detached house, stone built with a car park large enough for about four or five cars, designed to be purely operational for Belper town and local villages. The station I'd just left was at least ten times larger.

I arrived on the Monday morning and was greeted by the Station Sergeant, who was not really a sergeant but a retired one who had come out of retirement to man the station nine until five, Monday to Friday. He was a kindly and helpful man, as I was to discover, but ancient. The operational sergeant arrived soon after. A dour Scotsman if ever there was one, and difficult to understand.

We introduced ourselves and he immediately told me to put my cap on, get my suitcase and he would take me to my digs. My new home was a large six-bedroom stone farmhouse in a smallholding with sheep in the fields, a few cows in the large barn and chickens everywhere. I couldn't believe how grand it was, but I immediately recognised it. In my last year at school, I had taken part in a couple of Derbyshire schools' cross country competitions, and the route went down the side of this farmhouse, through their fields and along the river Derwent at the bottom of the small valley. We runners had been dropped off at the starting point and followed the route to the finish without ever seeing the town of Belper. Perhaps this was a good omen?

I carried my very heavy suitcase into the kitchen and was introduced to a woman who, over the next two years, would have a massive positive influence on my life. She became a mentor and mother-figure to me. She was very happily married to a loving husband who worked very hard in a highly-paid accountancy job in Derby, with grown up – well, 22 years old – twin sons, both farmers, and a young daughter. My new landlady, Mrs Meredith, was large and homely, smiley with an honest face and lovely. I think her second statement to me was along the lines that she would be giving me elocution lessons so that we could enjoy conversations both of us understood. I felt comfortable immediately.

I knew when I started writing these memoirs that I wouldn't name many names, because I had decided to dedicate them to the memory of Blanche Meredith (she's long been in heaven now), in honour of the debt I owe her and the esteem in which I hold her. Thank you, Mrs Meredith, for the hugs, especially the ones where I was enveloped so deeply that I couldn't be seen from the outside!

I'd never had a family hug. We weren't a family of touchy, feely, kissy types, until one of my sisters, Gaynor, followed in my footsteps, leaving home at the age of seventeen. She was blessed with the brains and the determination to go to university – also in the face of adversity. When she graduated, she went south and stayed there in the same way that I went north and never went back home. She was fourth in the line of our family of six children and we became best friends. We are touchy-feely and close. Gaynor has more brains than the rest of our family put together and is a shining example of what can be achieved through self-belief, determination and endeavour. We all knew she was special when as a three-year-old she could sing every verse of *Sailor Stop Your Roaming*, by Petula Clark, in front of an audience of neighbours. My other siblings grew up, left home and brought their own children up either living next door to my mam, next door but one, or within a couple of hundred yards. Notice no mention of dad there.

Dear Mrs Meredith, do you remember taking me into

the front room that no one used, sitting next to me and telling me that you believed I'd chosen the wrong career? You told me earnestly that I wasn't cut out to be a police officer and that I would make a much better nurse. I wasn't even offended! Your thoughts and considerations were always in my best interests. And I used to love it when you got up from the dinner table and clouted your twenty-odd year-old sons, who dwarfed even you, around the head every time they said, 'NNNNNick pppppass the bbbbbread and bbbbbutter!' They used to love it too, and how many times did it happen? Every meal time of course! You made me part of your family. You eventually helped people to understand my accent through your funny and warm elocution lessons and reduced my stutter further, to be more than manageable. I grew up quickly under your tutelage and I sincerely believe I am what I have become thanks to your guidance, care and belief – the nicer part of me, that is. Of course, my dad played a part in ensuring my path was diametrically opposed to his own, giving me the impetus and determination to be a worker and rally against injustice.

The police officers at Belper police station helped or hindered, swore at me or thanked me, belittled me or congratulated me as they prepared me for life as a constable. The most helpful were the ones who sometimes shared my digs, indeed my twin-bedded room, when they stayed, for whatever reason, for a couple of weeks or a couple of months.

I walked to and from work almost every day, through the fields and over the bridge, in less than 30 minutes. But I never walked as far as the beat bobbies. In those days they had to make half-hourly points at designated telephone boxes, so they could be contacted from the office and directed to whatever incident they had to deal with closest to their location. If the incidents were urgent they would stop a motorist and instruct the driver to take them there. It seemed everyone was prepared to help. Only the General Patrol Car had a radio, and that was so he could respond to incidents out in the sticks. Personal radios for police officers were still more than a year into the future. But it made for great policing and excitement as the Station Sergeant and I watched the clock tick down, enabling us to ring the designated public telephone box to direct a beat bobby to an incident. If there was no reply he would immediately be verbally accused by the elderly Station Sergeant, to me, of being in a pub somewhere. More often than not we would discover that a member of the motoring public had stopped and told him of an incident and transported him to the scene and he would already be dealing with it, or had dealt with it and moved on. Happy days!

21

SWIMMING WITH THE TIDE, FOR ONCE

Within weeks of my arrival at Belper, the swimming sergeant came to visit me and we sat for half a day discussing what the Chief Constable had said he wanted. This sergeant had been a keen and good swimmer in his time and was very enthusiastic about his instructions. It didn't take him long to make my days even happier. In those first few weeks, he drove me many times to Derby swimming baths to join in with a non-police lifesaving training class. I was soon going through my paces and showing others the best techniques in rescuing anyone from water.

On one memorable trip with him we went to a very important seminar on life saving at a university or college in Leicestershire. He picked me up from my digs at five o' clock in the morning, just as one of Mrs Meredith's recalcitrant twins was coming in from a girlfriend's house. We set off in the sergeant's new Vauxhall Viva. I left my digs with a warning from the errant son not to tell his mother what time he'd got home. No more stuttering stunts from him after that agreement.

There were a lot of life-saving representatives in the viewing area overlooking the swimming pool. Two excellent swimmers were demonstrating techniques, whilst one stood on the side talking us through what they were doing. They were also showing how many efforts to rescue a panicking drowning man resulted in both people drowning. They demonstrated the methods of approach and waiting, and how it was virtually impossible to take control of a man fighting for his life. During the lunch break my swimming sergeant told the organiser that his cadet would be able to rescue either of their men regardless of how they struggled. The challenge was accepted, to my dismay, and when everyone returned to the pool area to be told a challenge had been issued there was a sense of excitement from the watchers – and trepidation from me.

One of the men loaned me his trunks and stood on the side wrapped in a towel, while the other jumped in, swam to the middle of the pool and beckoned me in. There was no plan, just the swimming sergeant's belief in my ability. It didn't take long. I swam just out of his reach, round and round him as he tried to grab me. Eventually after one of his grabs just missed me I grabbed him, put my arm around his neck and with a good breath inside me took him under water, probably a bit longer than I should have done. When we surfaced, after getting his breath back he went wild. I wrapped my legs around his waist and my arm round his neck, tucked my chin in and just hung on as he flailed his arms and fists. He ran out of strength and towed him to the side with one arm across his chest and shoulder, to rapturous applause from the gallery and a big grin from his partner. For me it was another step in the right direction on my learning curve. Even some of the constables at my new police station heard about it and asked me to tell them what had happened. I loved it.

As the months went by my speaking voice slowed down and became more understandable. I grew in confidence and I was asked if I wanted to work shifts and man the police station on my own from six o'clock in the evening until ten o' clock at night. How could I say no? Unless there was a prisoner in one of the two cells at the back of the police station, of course. That didn't happen often, but when it did it offered me the opportunity of donning my cap and going into the main street to a local café to get his breakfast, lunch and evening meal. For me it was police work, not just shopping, but being on show to the public so they could see they were under my protection. Again, I loved it.

Of course not all the beat bobbies were of exemplary character. One I remember distinctly always smelled of beer, daytime and evening. He was the first one to take me out, in full uniform, on his beat. My 38-inch chest, which I could inflate a full three inches further with a deep breath, was puffed out in the glory and excitement of walking amongst the public, responding to their hellos and good mornings. By far the most popular comment, 'They get younger, don't they,' only made me smile more.

I was in my element until at one of our telephone box points, he smiled and told me we had been instructed to go to a sudden death at the local men's hostel. The manager showed us to a smelly bedroom and slumped behind the door was an old man, scruffy, with a beard and tobacco stained teeth. He was obviously dead, even to me, but the bobby told the residents and staff stood watching in the hallway that I was a trained life saver and that I would show them how to do mouth to mouth resuscitation just in case there was a chance of reviving him.

I was not just horrified, but petrified that I had been put in that position. I knew he was dead, his eyes had never blinked and there was no pulse in his carotid artery, but how could I refuse an order from a superior? I told him that I was sure he was dead and it was too late for resuscitation. In front of everyone he asked me if I was a doctor now and to at least give the man a chance. I took my handkerchief out to put over his mouth. I was immediately disappointed with myself. My handkerchief was not a pretty sight and since that moment of horror I have never left any of my homes without a clean handkerchief in my pocket.

I took my cap off, bent down and put my soiled handkerchief over his mouth. As I leaned over him, the beat bobby pulled me up off my knees and said he was just testing me. Judging by the looks on the faces of those watching, they were certain he hadn't been joking and their relief seemed as palpable as mine. He did do his job properly then though, as I watched him check the body, as he explained, for ligatures, stab wounds or any injuries that might mean a murder enquiry rather than death by natural causes.

We waited until the morticians arrived to take the body away. As we walked back to the police station for lunch, he explained that his job now was that of Coroners' Officer and he would be responsible for preparing the paperwork and attending the post-mortem on behalf of the coroner. He put his hand on my shoulder and told me I'd done well, that I'd seen enough death for one day and that I was too young to go to the mortuary with him. I didn't tell him.

I was never shy at running errands for any officer if it meant walking the streets of Belper in my uniform and I never turned down the offer of walking the streets in the company of the beat bobbies.

22

MEETING A MERMAID

██▼██▼██▼██▼██▼██▼██▼██▼

My swimming opportunities were increasing, and if I wasn't working a late shift, I was training most evenings at the pool in Derby. I was also being introduced to other police cadets who were potential members of the team and I trained them under the watchful eye of the swimming sergeant. Our team would consist of four with two reserves alternating into the team.

I was made captain of the team and our first competition at an indoor pool near Blackpool was almost an unmitigated disaster. There were eight or nine police forces taking part in a staged incident. All the teams waited in a locked room in a nearby building until the name of their team was called out. I led my team towards the pool entrance and was given a sheet of paper containing information about the incident. In this case it was a family picnic outing to a local beauty spot by the side of the river. Some of the family had been floating on a Li-Lo and had been blown off it. Some family members had jumped into the river to save them and become casualties themselves and in need of rescuing. The wind had blown a pram containing a six-month-old baby into the river. The current was strong and was flowing left to right. The ends of the pool were non-existent and therefore out of bounds. The last sentence advised us to rescue as many people as we could before the whistle went, and we were then to stop immediately

I read the scenario out loud to the team and then we were ushered into the pool area. The adrenaline and excitement caused by screams and shouts, splashing and cries of, 'I'm drowning!' and 'I've lost my baby!' prevented any of us looking up at the full viewing gallery. It was suddenly very real. I would be judged on my ability to lead and direct a successful outcome.

I knew from experience that I should assess the situation before deploying any of the team and that usually there would be some buoyancy aids and a rope or lengths of wood to assist in the rescue. The shouting and screaming was deafening and realistic. I looked up and down our side of the pool and saw some rope coiled on the other side of the river, which would necessitate someone swimming over to get it. I did however see the coiled high pressure fire hose hanging on the wall near the door we'd just entered from. I pulled the front of it and gave it to one of the team and told him to pull it into the water, and shouted at the six family members of various ages who were shouting, splashing and clinging to each other to grab hold of the hose and we'd pull them in. One woman was floating face down and obviously in immediate need of rescue. I sent one of the team to rescue her. He towed her back to the side and started pretend mouth-to-mouth. I held the mother back from jumping in where her baby had been lost. The other member of the team spotted the pram at the furthest point away from us in the opposite corner of the pool and rescued the doll. I didn't even have to get wet and was feeling quite pleased with myself.

We were filling in time resuscitating the people we had rescued until the timeout whistle went and it was then that I became aware of laughter from up above. I spotted my swimming sergeant with his head in his hands and as the adrenaline slowed down I started to wonder what on earth we had done wrong.

We were taken out to a hall to join those who'd taken part before us and wait until the other teams had finished. No one knew how any other team had performed, but it soon became apparent from our nervous discussions that I hadn't noticed the tarpaulin on our left-hand side higher up the river that hid some ropes and blankets. My first competition as captain of Derbyshire Police Cadets and I was admitting to the other captains that I'd missed the hidden aids and used the fire hose.

All the supporting cast, our respective leaders, guests and judges came into the hall. The judges sat on chairs on the stage and explained what had and what should have happened and also said they had made a mistake in not making the fire hose out of bounds. Cue much laughter, apart from my team and swimming sergeant. The results were read out from fourth place up and we came second, beaten by only one point. The judges said they couldn't fault my use of what aids there were available.

All the competitions we entered subsequently had brackets over the fire hoses and large signs saying 'DO NOT USE'. Although we never came first in any of them, we were always in the top three, usually second and I always found the correct life-saving aids. We had a very good team and were known wherever we went by many officers, regardless of rank. I was asked at most of the subsequent events by other captains to tell them exactly what happened with the fire hose. It didn't alter my attitude though. I was there to win at something I was very good at and I enjoyed every minute.

The training was fun if hard work, and it always attracted a lot of other swimmers to watch us at work, including the girl who became my first proper girlfriend since becoming a police cadet. Janet was a good swimmer and life saver, training at Derby baths and nothing to do with the police. She asked our swimming sergeant if she could do some life-saving training with us. We didn't have any girl cadets in our team, so we all voted immediately and energetically to let her join our training sessions. Most weeks she was my partner to rescue and I don't know if that was my luck or the Sergeant's design. When it came to swimming though, I suffered from a bit of tunnel vision and couldn't see the wood for the trees. After the training a group of as many as twenty of us would go to the pub opposite the pool sometimes and discuss in detail new techniques and swimming stories. She was invariably standing next to me in the group. Always lime and lemon for me of course and a soft drink for her.

After a couple of months even I began to realise that there was a romance in the making. We were becoming inseparable, in and out of the pool. I think I noticed when I chose to rescue her from 'drowning' and towed her by my arm across her chest, swimming side stroke method. Despite being shouted at by the sergeant to use the extended arm and chin towing method, she said it was all right to carry on – until we reached the end of the pool anyway and then I was told in no uncertain terms by the sergeant to do as I was told. It was a good thing he spoke to me, because it gave me the opportunity to stay in the pool until my erection subsided!

One of the older swimmers, from the private club of which my new friend was a member, obviously noticed the burgeoning romance going on between me and my belle. Some of them clubbed together to buy her a brandy and Babycham, known then as the 'knicker dropper'. It was all in good fun. One of them offered to let us use the back of his van in the car park. He made it seem more romantic when he told us there was a mattress in it. We sat in it for ages, both admitting we were virgins. When we went back to the pub with his keys we still were, but better kissers for the experience! But if I thought my first competition as Captain of Derbyshire Police Cadet Life Saving Team was embarrassing, my first attempt at lovemaking with my mermaid girlfriend was beyond comparison.

That wouldn't take place for quite a few months though. We were very content to meet after swimming, hold hands and kiss in any doorway. A mattress in a van was not in keeping with our virtues and standards, and nor was my BSA Bantam. My virginity and naivety were competing closely with one another.

23

DOG KILLER

My street walking in Belper was coming on apace, and if I wasn't sent to fetch food for the occasional prisoner, the beat bobbies had no qualms about sending me out to fetch and carry for them. I drew the line at purchasing cigarettes for any of them though. I abhorred the sight and smell of cigarettes and could retch at the sight of a full ashtray. Many of the officers smoked, but I stood my ground and refused to sit near them when they were smoking, despite being advised in colourful language that I should do what I was told.

One of my permanent jobs was to feed the stray dogs kept in the kennels compound at the back of the police station. Picking up their poo, or 'business', as we called it then, wasn't pleasant, but some of the dogs were adorable, so feeding and stroking them was a pleasure. Perhaps there was a conspiracy by some of the officers to thwart any possibility of continuous happiness, because as soon as I'd become attached to a poor dog it had to go. We only kept them for two weeks. If they hadn't been claimed by then they were taken away in a police car or van by two bobbies, to be destroyed.

One day I was ordered by the beat sergeant, Jennings, to accompany one of the bobbies to Heanor Police Station, about eight miles away, with one of the dogs due to be destroyed. I sat in the back of the police car with the mongrel, muzzled and on a lead. The bobby told me to tie the dog to a post at the back of the police station when we arrived. He showed me a large box, the size of a kennel. It had a hinged lid with a large wooden handle to one side, a hinged side panel with a metal tray and grill in the bottom. He told me to fill a bucket of water and pour it into the tray, then stand the dog in the box and close the door. He told me he would switch the power on and when I was sure everything looked OK with the dog, I was to close the lid and the dog would be electrocuted and killed.

I took the lead off him, took one last look at him, closed the lid and stood back. I heard sizzling and heard him fall down. No barking, no whimpering, just dead, or at least I hoped he was. Not that I wanted him dead, just not suffering. A minute later the bobby told me to pull the dog out and gave me a large heavy-duty plastic bag to put its body in. He went into the Police Station to telephone the council and tell them there was a dog's body to collect. It was nauseating. One minute stroking it to keep it calm and the next putting its body unceremoniously in a black bag. The only dignity afforded the poor thing was a seriously sympathetic police cadet in full uniform.

This procedure disturbed me and whenever we had a

stray dog in the station I always felt incredibly sorry for the poor creature as I fed and cleaned up after it. From then on, instead of using up two police officers' time off the street, I was always sent as the executioner. Over the following year I accompanied a driver on at least half a dozen occasions and was left to do the dirty work on my own and fill in the paperwork, whilst the bobby would talk to his colleagues in Heanor police station, have a cup of tea and make the necessary telephone call to the council to collect the dog's body. I treated this new experience seriously and respectfully and even though I didn't want to do it, I never made my feelings known. Even then I knew I would be faced with many worse situations in my career. And how right I was. Perhaps this was good grounding in a way for a seventeen-year-old. My nickname changed to 'The Executioner' for a while, but I never responded to that name, and that too died a death eventually.

It was all part of my learning curve. This kind of joshing is often referred to as 'gallows humour.' It's designed to help you hide your emotions, so you can get on with the job in extreme circumstances and to prevent yourself from becoming emotional or crying in front of the public. I'd long ago decided that no one was going to get the better of me. I would never allow any suggestion that I was not cut out to be a police officer. I did any job asked of me, professionally I believed, and always hid my anger or anxiety or self-pity. The time would soon come when I would be a regular police officer, and I knew I would never stoop to the level of some of the degradation I'd been subjected to by some officers. It was all part of my growing up and would help me in my crusade to prevent and fight injustice. Looking back though, I could probably have managed without quite a lot of the trials I was put through, and still achieved my aim of having a successful and memorable career in the police service.

On some occasions, for the odd night, week, or even a couple of months, police constables would stay in my digs. Many of them were friends of Mrs Meredith's sons and might have been on a night out with them — or one of her sons in particular. Some were having trial separations from their wives and others were on police training courses in Derby. I was mixing with regular police officers in a non-work environment, and it was a great experience. There was a certain amount of trust built up because of this and some of them taught me how to take witness statements, particularly from road traffic accidents or crimes such as theft or burglary.

One exceptional bobby gave me great advice (I found out many, many years later that he had had become a Chief Superintendent). He told me that when he read a statement I'd taken, he wanted to have a clear vision from start to finish, in chronological order, of exactly what the witness had seen, as if he was looking at the incident through their eyes. It was great advice and something I've passed on to hundreds of young police officers over the years. Many of the bobbies in Belper would make appointments for witnesses to call at the police station and ask for me so I could take their statements, although I was never allowed to countersign the statements. The officer involved in the case would eventually call in, read it, thank me and sign it as if he'd taken it.

My learning curve was huge, relevant, and personal and I loved it. It was a great experience and everyone complimented me on my handwriting, which was then described as copperplate writing. I was trusted and regularly thanked and congratulated. This certainly made up for my lack of 'O' Level English.

If I was on the occasional late shift, I would have a whole morning with Mrs Meredith, talking, listening and learning the benefits of always being honest, hardworking, helpful, respectful, and considerate and all the other attributes she believed a young man should have. I was a sponge for her advice and training. She told me she wanted to be proud of me. I would sometimes tell her stories of my childhood and she would suddenly get up and envelope me in one of her huge bear hugs as if she was trying to erase my memories. I'd never discussed any of my childhood memories with anyone before, but it seemed so natural to talk to her, and to be honest, I loved the bear hugs. Mrs Meredith told me that one day I must bring my mam to meet her.

24

MOBILITY, A NERVOUS BREAKDOWN AND GRANDMA'S PRIDE

■▬■▬■▬■▬■▬■▬■▬■▬■▬■▬■▬

On one of my many visits to Derby for cadet or swimming training, I walked past a showroom and saw my first car. Not exactly a car; it had three wheels and a motorbike engine mounted on the front wheel under the bonnet. It was a two-seater Bond Mini Car. I knew from all my police law book reading that it was classed as a motorcycle because it had fewer than four wheels and weighed less than eight hundredweight. I could drive it on my motorbike licence, without 'L' plates. I went back the following day on my own little BSA Bantam and asked how much it would cost, with my bike as part exchange and paying monthly. I was told I needed a guarantor and the salesman suggested my dad. I suggested my uncle and he agreed.

I rode to Grassmoor, where my Uncle Gordon lived and

after a bit of persuading he agreed to be my guarantor. A week later I picked him up as pillion passenger and took him to the showroom to sign for my new steed. It was a 1960 model, dark green, with an aluminium body and a beige glass fibre roof — a keep-you-dry motorbike! It had a Villiers 250cc two-stroke engine mounted on the front wheel. The wheel turned 90 degrees so a reverse gear wasn't necessary – it turned on its own axis. The alternative description allocated to it by Mrs Meredith was a 'potential death trap'. I was the first in my family of uncles, aunts and cousins to drive behind a steering wheel, except the uncle who beat up my dad. He was a lorry driver.

The difficult part for my uncle came when the salesman asked me what driving experience I had. He was rather astonished when I told him just motorbikes. To my uncle's obvious terror, the salesman gave me a lesson in the car park at the back of the showroom. The shop was just about to close as it was five o' clock. He showed me the handle on the steering column that changed the gears just as a foot pedal did on a bike, up and down the gears, but the clutch, brake and accelerator were operated the same as a car. His most memorable bit of advice was to be careful going up a long hill as the petrol to the carburettor was gravity fed and it might run out of fuel!

After about ten minutes I persuaded my uncle to get in the passenger seat and off we went in the general direction of Chesterfield, in high volume tea-time traffic. I stalled it often. We went through traffic lights at red because they were on green when I stalled it. We went into wrong lanes at roundabouts, sometimes circling them and at others going down side streets to turn around to rejoin the main road. I don't know how many times my uncle tried to get out, but I do know that he spent most of the journey with a white face, his arms horizontal in front of him and his hands pressed against the bottom of the windscreen, shouting out whenever we were near a lorry and its wheels were higher than his head. It wasn't funny, even for me. It's safe to say that I was as wet as I would have been if I'd been swimming fully clothed, which I did regularly in life-saving training, but on this occasion I didn't smell of chlorine.

But in the end it was worth it. After thirty or so miles I'd taught myself to drive, taught my uncle never to trust me again, dropped him off at home a nervous wreck and set off confidently to my grandma's to show her my pride and joy. She never went in it, but laughed for years when she regaled me with my uncle's version of events.

On this visit she also showed me a copy of the weekly *Derbyshire Times*, her local weekly newspaper, in which there was a photograph of me as group leader of the Derby County and Borough Police Cadet expedition team to Snowdonia. There were other cadets in the photo, but I was at the front. I hadn't told her about the expedition, but she said it was hard to believe that I could be in the pages of *The Times* and be the leader of the police cadets. She said she was so proud. So was I. I'd thought the photograph session was for police records, not a newspaper, so I'd never told her about it. She told me she loved going to the shops when her neighbours would talk to her about me and she would tell them what I was up to.

When I drove to my digs in Belper the next day I was of course ridiculed by the Meredith twins and most of the bobbies at the police station when I parked it next to the police cars, but I was ecstatic. After a couple of days of magnificent independence, I picked my mermaid up from Derby to show her where I worked and lived. I'd become a very competent driver in a couple of days, and knew the car's limits. I drove her up the hill of the main road through Belper town to the main junction and stopped first in line at the traffic lights. Unbeknown to her, whilst talking, I turned the steering wheel ninety degrees to the right. When the lights changed to green and the line of traffic set off downhill towards us I let the clutch out and my car turned on its own axis, just managing to take the lead of the line of vehicles coming *down* the hill. She screamed as the first car headed straight at her, honking its horn, as she tried to climb over my left shoulder. Anyway, I thought it was hilarious.

25

A FUMBLED ENCOUNTER, AND A SERIOUS SCOLDING

My girlfriend got her own back shortly afterwards, but not with malice aforethought. I took her to my digs when Mrs Meredith was out and the house empty. I took her to my room, because it was simply apparent that we were going to lose our virginity. I should have heeded Mrs Meredith's words of advice about being, amongst others, respectful and considerate. It wasn't my house and if I'd wanted to take anyone to my room in their house, as Mrs Meredith's husband put it so sternly that evening, I must always ask permission, which might, or might not, be granted. That part of the episode hurt me because I'd been caught out as disloyal and disrespectful. Typically though, they forgave me and I had another bear hug – and a firm handshake from Mr Meredith, but with a cautionary wag of his finger.

Being caught out like that hurt my pride, but it was nowhere near as embarrassing as lying on top of my girlfriend kissing her passionately on my bed, trying without success to get my willy in. I did no preparation for my big event, other than the foreplay of kissing. I didn't have a condom and was about to ejaculate. I got off, stood up and looked down at her. She was smiling, in a genuinely loving way, and pointed to her nether regions as she told me she still had her knickers and tights on. I've heard plenty of comedians tell similar stories over the years, but this was true. It was 1968 and I was seventeen years old.

We remained friends, but never again attempted to be lovers. I wanted to tell Mrs Meredith and her husband when they were chastising me that nothing had happened, but would they have believed me? I'd betrayed their trust, so it was irrelevant anyway. And anyway, what would my life have been like if the twins had known of my abject failure?

Mrs Meredith forgave me and carried on treating me as someone special. I think I was somewhere between a son and pupil in her eyes. I redoubled my efforts to please, helping more around the house and finding eggs in areas of the barn not visible to the human eye.

Another abiding memory of being out in my Bond Mini Car was with my mermaid en- route to a party at her friend's house near Derby. I stupidly stalled the engine. The key ignition start had been broken for a few weeks and I had to open the bonnet, get my leg over the inside of the engine compartment to reach the kick start whilst holding the bonnet up and start the engine like a normal motorbike. Having to face the ignominy of doing this in front of your passenger, not to mention your girlfriend, or any passing motorist, really made sure you never stalled the car. On this occasion it was dark and raining and I was wearing my first-ever suit, a charcoal grey three-piece with flared trousers. The flare of my right trouser leg caught on the fins above one of the pistons, which tore it open along the inside seam, up to my knee. The whole trouser leg was flapping around. I wanted to go back home, but my girlfriend insisted she was looking to show me off to her friends. Everything worked once a dozen or so safety pins had fastened the trouser leg together, and the party was good. Punk rockers eat your hearts out. I was there fifteen years before you!

On one of my now regular full uniform walks on my own, to do the shopping, I always stopped to talk to an elderly man who would lean on his gate as I walked past. He was complimentary and pleasant, but I noticed that he walked to and from his gate in obvious pain, on two walking sticks. I always asked after his health and in particular about his discomfort when walking, until one day, after some weeks, he told me he would like to share a secret with me, but he was very embarrassed about it.

In the front room of his little terraced house, facing the main street used by hundreds of people every day, he let me into his secret over a cup of tea. He pulled one of his slippers off and showed me his foot. His toe nails were black, but had grown so long for so long that they had curled under his toes and into the back of the flesh. Some of them were so huge that they dug into the balls of his feet. No wonder he was in agony. They weren't toenails that could be cut with nail scissors, or even kitchen scissors, because I had a go there and then. They were thick and ugly. I asked if I could take him to the doctor's, but he said he didn't do doctors, and he would stay in his house until he died. He repeatedly told me how embarrassed he was, but he didn't have any family and couldn't walk as far as the doctor's on his own. His meagre supplies were brought to him by an elderly neighbour living next door. He had never told her what was causing his lack of mobility.

I should have arranged for a doctor to visit, but he said all the right words about trusting me and not to embarrass him further. I returned the next day with some household wire cutters and over a period of about two weeks snipped away until all his nails were cut and pulled out of the flesh. We used cotton wool, plasters and disinfectant and the relief after a couple more weeks was heartbreaking to see. He was walking to the shops a few weeks later, hobbling but not in pain. He was so appreciative that I ended up being embarrassed by his effusiveness and stopped going in for tea, contenting myself with talk at his garden gate, or in the street when he was shopping.

I tried to keep his secret to myself, but I couldn't resist telling one of the bobbies what I had been doing on my shopping trips. I was referred to by many at the station as 'the Chiropodist', or 'the Footman.' Mrs Meredith called me an angel, again in one of her bear hugs.

26

CHESHIRE HOME

■.■.■.■.■.■.■.■.■.■.■.■.■.■.■.■.

I wasn't seeing much of my handlebar-moustachioed fighter pilot Chief Inspector of Cadets now I was working at a different police station, but when I went to Derby for training, he would sometimes call into the classroom. He would always speak to me and tell me the life-saving team was doing very well and to keep up the good work.

On one of these training days he gave us a talk on our responsibilities and how lucky we were not to be working down the mines, or in factories or hospitals. He told us that we needed to appreciate what we had. To remind us of how tough the world was for others, he had arranged for some or all of us to visit and work in other workplaces. We were all going to Markham Colliery near Chesterfield, where we would go down in a cage to see the coalface. He said it would help us understand why miners liked to have a few beers on their days off, and we should take this into account when we qualified to be constables. I don't think I knew the word 'irony' at that point in my life.

We all went down the shaft, including the girl cadets, and we were treated with genuine respect by the men working above and below ground. My dad worked, occasionally, at this pit, but of course I didn't see him, as he was what the other miners would call 'a narrow-back' or work-shy, and I certainly didn't tell my colleagues about my family.

I received my written instructions to spend a month in a Leonard Cheshire home near Ashby de la Zouch, and the following two months in Derby Royal Infirmary. My instructions to start at the Leonard Cheshire Home, where the patients suffered from multiple sclerosis, advised that I was to work the hours set by the manager, five days a week, but it was my choice if I wanted to stay there seven days a week.

I was dropped off by police car at the entrance to a beautiful old stone-built manor-type house. The approach was down a winding gravel lane through manicured gardens and massive imposing trees. I half expected to be greeted by a butler at the top of the steps. Instead I was greeted by a nurse and taken to my room to drop my suitcase off, then told to leave my tunic and cap in the room and come back down for lunch. No patients anywhere. I was introduced to various nursing-type staff, all of whom were very pleasant, but there was nothing inspiring to see other than the beautiful building, its ornate classical interior and surrounding gardens. What a contrast I was about to witness!

Eventually I was given a white lab coat and taken to a ward housing about a dozen male patients, or residents, some of whom were in wheelchairs and others bedridden. There were other wards or rooms where patients lived. I'd never heard of multiple sclerosis and I was shocked to see the state these patients were in, with their bodies, hands and heads in twisted shapes. I followed my allocated nurse around, picking things up and handing things to her as she fed the patients, and stood by as she changed their clothing, took them to the toilet or dealt with their bedpans and generally cared for the poor souls. When I picked a plastic beaker up next to one patient, she shouted at me to come back - just as he lashed out and hit the side of my head with the back of his hand. She told me he was always angry and lashed out at everyone and to be careful. I followed her around dutifully for the rest of the day.

After a couple of days lifting, carrying and passing, looking helplessly and embarrassingly at the poor patients, I was convinced that I would contract multiple sclerosis myself at some stage of my life. They were living a twenty-four-hour-a-day nightmare and by the end of the first week I was sharing their pain and despair. I slowly got to know their names and could make out the odd word or two, and eventually I understood what they wanted and what I could do to help.

John, the angry patient, was only in his fifties, and still strong and well-built at this stage of his illness. I started to talk to him whenever I was dealing with another patient, without getting too close to him. He couldn't talk back, but eventually he let me feed him and change his clothing. I found he'd been a dentist or a doctor. His eyes flamed with anger or passion and sometimes he would cry or shout unintelligible words and froth at the mouth, his body shaking in his wheelchair.

As I got to know him, and he started to trust me — and

stopped trying to hit me — I would tell him stories about my own life and some of the silly things I'd done, but also about my swimming. Sometimes he would laugh, and the nursing staff said they'd never seen that before. He never had any visitors and sometimes he looked so sad that I would just sit and talk to him or read to him for hours. I believe all the other patients had visitors regularly, and at these times I felt sad for him.

In the middle of the second week a wonderful thing happened. There were quite a few volunteers who came for a few hours at a time, morning, afternoon or evening. They would sit with patients reading newspapers and helping to feed some of them. If any of these volunteers approached my Mr Angry he would soon react and push them away, indicating he wanted me to be with him. But on this particular day we were both immediately smitten by the most beautiful girl in the world, probably. Long blonde hair, blue eyes, freckles, pouty lips, dimples and a sweet and ready smile. I must have stared at her for a long time, because she looked up at me at least four or five times before Mr Angry tenderly hit me on my head with the back of his hand, making noises that I knew were laughter.

This girl of every man's dreams took the initiative and came over to talk to me. She spoke confidently and told me she had been a volunteer for six months. She said she'd heard they were getting some police cadets to help out and was pleased to meet me. I agreed I was a police cadet, but I wasn't sure I was exactly helping. She came in every day that week and we tentatively spoke more and more. She came in on the Saturday and said she was surprised to see me working the weekend. When I told her I wasn't going home, she invited me to her house for tea and said her parents wouldn't mind if I stayed the night in the spare room. If they did mind her brother would bring me back after tea.

Again my lack of manners and social graces let me down. I met her family and they could not possibly have been more welcoming and friendly. I had tea, bed and breakfast and walked miles in their beautiful village with their beautiful daughter, including calling at her dad's garage where she showed me the light blue Austin Healey 2000 sports car her dad had bought for her to renovate. All this in a quaint little village, occupied and lived in by genuine, pleasant, loving families. These nice houses with their lovely gardens surrounded by fields were not somewhere I belonged. I did not take my eyes off Miss World until we went back to the Cheshire Home the next day and started work, but the experience was, selfishly, good for me. Did I thank her parents? Did I buy her mum some flowers or her dad a bottle of wine? Did I do anything to endear them to me, or anything to make them believe their daughter had found a nice lad? I'm afraid not. They were more likely to remember my ignorance.

I grew in confidence working with the patients, but my favourite was always Mr Angry. I was allowed to feed him, and undress and dress him ready for bed or his wheelchair. We laughed together when I told him silly jokes. He loved it when I was emptying or changing his catheter and made jokes about what a waste his willy was. One of the funniest moments we had was when I was taking the bag of urine away and noticed a grey mass of foreign bodies floating in it. I was genuinely concerned and showed it to a nurse as she walked by. She wasn't flustered at all and said that he must have been masturbating in his sleep. I was flustered enough for the three of us when she told me this.

As I washed his nether regions, I picked his willy up

between my finger and thumb and congratulated him that it was still working. I asked him who he had been thinking of during the night and just at that moment Miss World walked into our ward. He almost jumped out of his chair, thrashing about and laughing, his eyes shining wildly with humour. He kept waving one hand at her, making unintelligible noises and making it quite obvious she was the woman of his dreams — as she was mine! I collapsed into his wheelchair with him and we couldn't stop laughing, despite enquiring looks and questions from the staff. I kept his secret throughout my stay there, but we often talked about her at night when I was putting him to bed. At least I talked, while he made it very obvious he was in full agreement, rocking backwards and forwards, shaking one hand. But his eyes were the giveaway. They shone and sparkled. If he did have any family, they should have seen him like that. It was only his body that was broken.

My stay at this Cheshire Home was mostly a sad experience, and the highlight was my brief association with Miss World, but my time spent with Mr Angry put my life and everything else into perspective. It made me understand why I had been sent there, and why I hoped, fervently, that I would never be in such an institution as a patient. Such are the injustices of the world we live in. What a character he was. I wondered what kind of life he had led for his family to ignore him in his time of need. I regularly compared his life with my dad's and thought of the imbalance.

But my life had to move on. I was shortly due at Derby Royal Infirmary for my introduction to another workplace. I left Mr Angry with regret, and it was a sorrowful parting. But I still hadn't learned enough about manners and social graces, because, I'm sorry to say, I never went back to visit him. I so wish I had, but my excuse was that I was on such a fantastic learning curve in life that I could only bring myself to look forward. My present and future were so exciting, and I was selfish. I was also seventeen.

I had a week at my grandma's after my Mr Angry and Miss World experience and spent some time with my siblings, but I missed work and preferred being there. I was addicted to my future and the potential for excitement. There were times of course when I was embarrassed or upset by the behaviour of some of my colleagues towards me, but overall my determination to learn, succeed and progress was overwhelming and I could not afford to waste a day.

The next chapter of my young life which the Chief Inspector of Cadets had arranged for me was designed to further open my eyes and see at first-hand how nursing staff worked and lived. This meant two months at DRI. I might have been naïve, but I was receptive, and I always appreciated what other people were doing to live their lives through work and play. I'd been to Chesterfield Hospital a few times. Once it was to check if a lead bomber plane had removed my left eye, as referred to earlier, and once to set my broken arm in plaster after cycling into the path of a motorbike and sidecar, before my age had reached double digits. I'd been born in the hospital too, so I suppose that was three times. The only other hospital I'd visited was to see my dad weave baskets, if it was indeed a hospital. With so many locked doors I'm sure that one wasn't for repairing physical injuries.

Try and consider a spectrum, and how extreme one end could possibly be from the other. That was my experience of DRI compared with the Leonard Cheshire Home. On arrival I was told by a Sister that I was to spend my two months in the Accident and Emergency Department. I was introduced to numerous female and male nurses in their A&E staff room. They were boisterous and good fun, and as I learned during my time there they were very dedicated. I swapped my tunic and cap for a long white coat but still wore my blue shirt, black tie, serge trousers and boots.

It didn't take me long to realise I had an aptitude for the kind of work carried out by these nursing staff. I started off with portering duties, and the sight of blood and obvious agony of the patients as I wheeled them from one place to another did not upset me or detract from my overall interest in their medical progress. I was at the beck and call of everyone, but I did everything with enthusiasm. I was courteous and respectful and found it very easy to speak with frightened patients on trolley beds in my care and have conversations with those who were bullish about their predicaments.

The staff worked shifts, so in my time there I met all of them, as I worked roughly from nine until five or six. Mr Meredith dropped me off most days on his way to work. I saw a few of the nurses a lot more than others, and built up bonds with most of these. I was accepted into their inner ring and included in their conversations on likes and dislikes, boyfriends and girlfriends and nights out. The only thing I didn't do was visit the smoke room with them.

The Sister who was in charge took a particular interest in me, and whenever she went to see a patient she took me with her. I was her shadow for the best part of two months. She always introduced me as a trainee doctor, and this brought many giggles from other nurses. I watched her give injections, put stitches in and take stitches out, and once I saw her slice the sides of a man's big toe to remove an ingrowing toenail. She was unshakable. Nothing and no one got the better of her. She was a natural leader, and I admired her.

The laughter and stories at tea and meal breaks with the nurses were always great fun, but much of it was not stuff you'd tell your grandmother about. Nurses share the same gallows humour as police officers, and there seemed to be no secrets.

One of the male nurses was very good fun, good at his job and good looking, and he asked me to have a night out with him. He came to Belper, picked me up from my digs and we went to a country pub nearby. He soon cottoned on that we weren't suited, so we shook hands and he dropped me off shortly afterwards. He had made the mistake of misjudging my sexuality, and I reminded myself how naive I was. We still had a great relationship at the hospital, as though nothing had happened. He was a lovely young man who cared passionately about the work he was doing.

In my second month, my favourite nursing sister told me that I had now witnessed her take hundreds of stitches out and that I was more than capable of doing it myself. She'd taught me how to thread the needle and wrap bandages around fingers, arms and legs, so I was an able assistant most of the time. It never occurred to me to refuse and I was excited when she supervised my first efforts, congratulating me as I competently did what she'd taught me. It was simple enough so long as you made sure, after cutting the gut,that you pulled the stitch out from the end with the knot in it and didn't try and pull the knot through the flesh. I became sufficiently proficient that she would start me off and then leave me alone with the patient in a curtained-off cubicle. This wonderful lady of the lamp and leader of nurses also showed me how to give tetanus injections, only in men's thighs of course, but I had no qualms.

Some of the other nurses knew what their boss was doing with me and told me I was a natural. They suggested I should leave the police and be a nurse. My friendly male nurse clapped and gave me a hug at this suggestion. Mrs Meredith had spotted this a lot earlier, but it was never going to happen. I knew where my future lay, even though many others didn't share my self-belief and optimism.

27

A MEDICAL LIFE-CHANGER

My most memorable medical moment came in my final week at the DRI. My friendly sister told me a man had been brought in with a gash in his knee and she wanted me to deal with him from start to finish. He was a builder's labourer, heavily built, and had knelt on a broken bottle. She told me, in front of her staff, that I was to clean the man's wound, inject a local anaesthetic straight into the open wound, thread the needle and stitch it up.

The wound was a ninety-degree cut, like a capital letter 'L'. One length of the cut was about one inch long and the other one and a half inches. She told me I needed to insert seven or eight stitches and finish it off with a tetanus injection, and she would inspect my work and do the bandaging. She told him that he should have a neat scar at the end of it. She also told him to be more careful in future.

I really wasn't ready for this, mentally, but he was sitting on the bed waiting and my lady of the lamp had given me confidence. She passed me the phial of anaesthetic and I loaded the syringe. She watched me insert it into his flesh and paid particular attention that I pulled the syringe back a little to make sure there was no blood in it —- that I wasn't about to inject into a vein. She said that was good and told me to inject.

She left the curtained cubicle, and as I pushed the needle containing the anaesthetic into his wound I went a bit light-headed and started sweating. The sweat changed the colour of my shirt, and I imagine my face too. The sweat was dripping off the end of my nose and chin, and he started to panic. I couldn't blame him. He shouted for the nurse and asked me if I was sure I was a doctor. The lady of the lamp came in like a whirlwind, berating him in a loud voice that of course I wasn't a doctor, that I was a trainee. When he pointed to my boots and serge trousers and asked if I was a porter, she was all fire and brimstone and told him to behave like a man and not a baby.

My nursing mentor stayed with me, watching my ministering closely, and to my astonishment everything went to plan. The stitches were neat and there was no bleeding – just some damp salty sweat marks on his leg. When my angel nurse congratulated me and bandaged his knee, he apologised to her and shook my hand. Those were the days! If anything ever could be designed to give a young man a boost in confidence,that was it. I was delighted and proud of myself and loved the company of the nurses.

Mrs Meredith reiterated her claim that I should consider a career in nursing, but I think she was a bit sceptical of my story. I didn't blame her, and I still find it hard to believe myself. But I was a bit of a hero in the A&E Department and I loved it. I couldn't do it now though — even if I was allowed!

My most memorable non-medical moment came on my last day at the hospital. I was told a cake had been brought in and everyone was going to give me a good farewell at the end of the day. One of the nurses I'd spent time with was pretty but not as loud as the others. She had brown hair and brown eyes, and she was lithesome and quite a few years older than me. We were alone at the tea point and she asked me if I ever had sexual fantasies. There was nothing I could say to that – in fact I was speechless. She told me she had a fantasy, and as it was my last day she wanted me to help her. She told me to follow her, and led me to a row of offices in the corridor, where the top half of the glass was see-through and the bottom half painted dark cream. She led me by the hand into one of the offices and locked the door behind us. Then she pushed my back against the window, unfastened and pulled down my serge trousers and gave me what I later found out was called a blow job. It was incredible and frightening at the same time. I could hear people walking down the corridor directly behind me and porters wheeling patients on trolleys as I stared, petrified, at the table and chairs, wall charts and full-size plastic skeleton propped against the wall opposite me. I wanted to look down to see what the whole procedure looked like, but I didn't dare.

It didn't take long, and I'm still not sure if that was fortunate or unfortunate. Suddenly she was pulling my trousers back up and we were both fumbling to fasten them. I remained bolt upright to avoid any suspicions among those in the corridor only inches behind my back as she was kneeling down in front of me. My heart was pounding so loud I'm surprised it didn't stop or that someone in the corridor didn't hear it.

When my trousers and white coat were fastened, she stood up in front of me. I still hadn't spoken a word since she had asked me if I would help with her sexual fantasy. I looked into her face and she had a half-smile and a sparkle in her eyes. I was ready to faint as the adrenaline started to slow down. She pointed with one finger to her puffed-out cheeks and indicated for me to go back to the tea point and nurses' lounge.

I was in a complete and utter state of shock and felt like running away to avoid facing the other nurses as I walked back down the corridor in the midst of hospital staff and members of the public. Most of the nursing staff I worked with were already there, talking, drinking tea and orange juice and eating cake, and everyone welcomed me. When my fantasist came into the room a short time later, flushed as I recollect, my angel in charge nurse asked her where she'd been, and said we'd started without her. She smiled and said she'd been to clean her teeth.

I couldn't look at her because I knew my face was bright red. There was plenty of chatter, all good-natured, congratulations on the work I'd done over the past two months, handshakes, cheek kissing, hugs, a particularly long one from my male nurse friend, and a kiss on my lips from my angel mentor before I was allowed to leave. I tried to avoid eye contact with the fantasist, but every time I looked at her she was smiling directly at me and all I could do was wish I'd watched what she had been doing. I avoided going up to her to say goodbye because I think I would have collapsed.

My virginity was almost gone and I left the hospital on a massive high. So many things had happened to significantly change my life during my work experience there. It had been a fantastic experience, and so enjoyable and memorable. Much, much later I wondered if it was just my fantasist and I who knew what had happened in the skeleton's office on my last day. Or had I been set up again? Perhaps they had drawn lots. I'm fantasising now!

28

A SLAPPED FACE

My life was blooming, or at least budding, and the instruction I now received from my Chief Inspector that I was soon to start a month's police driving course was the icing on my cake. I already had my provisional car licence, so a week later I reported for driving instruction at the road traffic department, half a mile up the steep hill from Matlock Police Station. There were twelve of us, with four cars and an instructor for each car at our disposal. I was the only cadet, the others being regular officers either being taught to drive or on a refresher. If you are not old enough to remember Ford V6 Zephyrs and Zodiacs, please Google them. They were, at that time, state-of-the-art four-door saloons used by our Traffic Department. They were monsters, with leather bench seats, the gear stick on the column and, in capable hands, fast. The engine was the equivalent of twelve times the size of the one that powered my Bond Mini Car.

I'd always been a bit crazy riding my bikes flat out around bends, banking over so the foot pedal scraped the road, so getting into cars like these was not daunting, just exciting. The police sergeant instructors carried a twelve-inch ruler in their right hand at all times and even the tiniest error resulted in a slap on your left thigh. With no notice he might suddenly ask for the colour of the car behind and at the same time cover the rearview mirror up with his hand. A delay in answering or a wrong answer resulted in a sharp slap with his ruler. If we signalled too early or too late it meant another slap. Our thighs became sorely bruised after a week. We were taught to thank approaching motorists who had done a good deed, perhaps flashing to let us pull out, by saluting them, but with our left hands. We were instructed that a salute, even left handed, is more appropriate for a police driver than a wave. It was explained that the motorist opposite us could not see a right-handed salute.

The pleasantest and most professional sergeant at Belper, Sergeant Rose, deserves a mention about saluting, if only to give balance to some of his meaner colleagues. He took me for a walk through the town on a few occasions and asked about my life, my family and swimming and showed a genuine interest. Of course I never mentioned anything about the domestic side of my life to him. On one of these walks with him he told me in a sharp tone to stand to attention at the side of him as a funeral cortege was passing. He stood firmly to attention and saluted. I followed suit and he whispered to me not to, as it was courtesy for only the senior officer to salute. What a lovely man. For years I copied his manners whenever a cortege was passing and have had some rewarding nods of appreciation from families following the hearse.

During my month's driving course, every morning was classroom work and the afternoon dedicated to driving. I loved both. Before we could drive off we were told what order we would be driving in. The three drivers had to stand at the side of their nominated driver's door and the other two at the rear passenger doors. The instructors watched us like hawks as we marched to our respective positions. We had to practise opening them at the same time and closing them in unison. If one car door out of the twelve was not in sync, everyone had to get out and start again until it was perfect. The nominated driver would then have to get out and check the oil, water and tyre pressures under the watchful eye of the instructor before the driving lessons commenced. This was okay the first week because it was still exciting, although after that it became tedious. But we were all in awe, or in my case a bit frightened, of the instructors, so no one spoke up or questioned their orders.

In the final week I did make a suggestion and was slapped across the face, quite hard too, by the policewoman traffic officer, who was on her refresher course. Part of the training was to stop close behind the vehicle in front of us on hills, so that if the car in front had difficulty carrying out a hill start and rolled back, the damage would be minimal. You could see the panic in the eyes of the driver in front when we pulled up behind, obviously police officers, and this often caused them to stall their car and panic even more. I suggested in the classroom session that if we stayed further back it would give the driver in front more confidence so that they would be less likely to stall, and if it did roll back we wouldn't be close enough to be hit before the driver braked and stopped.

The instructor left the classroom immediately and the policewoman came over to me. She asked me who I thought I was and told me I 'was only a cadet.' Then, without further ado, she slapped me across the face. Before anyone had time to react, the instructor came back in and told us he'd discussed what I'd said to the other instructors and they all agreed that from this day on we would try it. The policewoman burst into tears and ran out of the classroom. The instructor asked what was going on and everyone looked at me. He asked me directly what had happened. I told him nothing had happened.

We all went off for the practical driving and fortunately for me, probably, my assaulter was in a separate car. The next morning in front of the whole class she came over, said she was sorry and shook my hand. She treated me as an equal and indeed was quite friendly for the remainder of the course. My recommendation on hill starting was implemented on all subsequent driving courses. I passed with flying colours and made the instructor laugh when I said if I ever won the pools I would come back and buy the Zodiac I'd been driving.

29

GOODBYE VIRGINITY AT LAST

My cadetship was coming up to its final year, but of course eighteenth birthdays were no big occasion, other than for buying a legal round in a pub. Despite the fears and frights I'd been subjected to I was now growing into a confident young man.

I was still a virgin in the literal sense of the word, but that was just about to change. I knew one of the girl cadets based in Derby fancied me, but I'd been warned off her by a few of my colleagues. She had a great sense of humour though and always made me laugh. After one particularly ribald comment she made in the classroom, I decided I was going to go out with her. One of our cadets in the classroom that day, a particularly beautiful, bright and sophisticated girl, obviously not my type, asked to leave the classroom as she felt faint. No sooner had she left the room than my soon-to-be-amour told everyone that it was morning sickness. Everyone clamoured at the same time, asking who the father was, or offering their suggestions as to who they thought the lucky person might be. My soon-to-be-beau commented in a loud voice that if you eat a plate of peas how do you know which ones make you fart? Even the sergeant instructor laughed at that. These were the days of Bruce Forsyth, Tony Hancock and Morecambe and Wise, so 'gutter humour' was a long way off, but she was a natural. I was so impressed I asked her out that evening and she said she'd love to.

I picked her up in my three-wheeler that night and we went into the hills. She'd turned down my offer of going for a drink, telling me that if it was sex I was after, we could have a drink later. Crossing your legs in my three-wheeler was difficult, so losing your virginity in an embrace was almost impossible and of course the seats didn't recline. She chatted and was her humorous self in the build-up to my anticipated magical moment, which helped keep me calm. The kissing was good, but when the time came to make the physical moves we found it was impossible. We were both athletic enough, but if it wasn't for my pure determination to succeed and her eventual agreement to open her passenger door, we could have ended up in hospital. About a minute later that's exactly what I was thinking about – hospital and baby.

I was in a complete state of panic about performing, but happy that I'd witnessed her undressing her lower half, knowing I wasn't going to feel any fabric obstacles spoiling my moment of glory. Two pairs of bare legs (my skinny ones identified by shoes on and trousers round my ankles) sticking out of one side of a shaky three-wheeler could have caused it to tipple over onto us, but I was beyond caring. It certainly didn't leave much to the imagination for passers-by. I pushed it in, with some guidance, felt the extreme heavenly pleasure, excitement, physical and mental warmth and gratitude, and then she told me as I got started that if I got her pregnant she'd know who to come to – and that I'd have to marry her. I didn't just pull out, I leapt out, and then watched as my second-ever ejaculation in the presence of a woman shot out of me. In this case it was onto her legs and the inside of the door. She sat up and asked me if this was my first time, and did I want to wait a bit and have another go. At least I had a clean handkerchief this time to repair some of the damage.

She was still full of humour, and my disastrous attempt at being a passionate lover didn't upset her. She was kind enough to tell me it would be better if we used a bed next time. I was too mortified at the thought of being a husband and a father at the age of eighteen, and not fulfilling my dream of being a policeman, to even consider another attempt.

I thanked my lucky stars, for her words spoken at the perfect moment, my speed of reaction to prevent a tragedy and also for her help in losing my virginity, such as it was. Parenthood and marriage could wait. I'd wanted my loss of virginity to be a success and I was disappointed with myself. I'd held on to it for long enough and now it was gone in two thrusts. I realised my target of becoming a good policeman wasn't the only target I needed. I determined to plan the sex side of my life a lot better and next time at least have one condom in my pocket. The next time wasn't much better as it turned out, again outdoors, on grass, but at least it would be with my future wife, and we could learn together.

30

THE KICK THAT THREATENED MY CAREER

Within a couple of weeks of this sad episode in my life, all my hard work, commitment and enthusiasm to be a police officer almost vanished, because of one of my spur-of-the-moment actions. It was so serious that I deserved to be sacked as a police cadet. But it was something I couldn't control, and I didn't have time to consider the consequences when it started.

I'd driven to my old school for gym training and decided to call in on my grandma, unannounced. Contact with my family, other than by my personal visits, was always done by letter. When I opened my grandma's back door I was shocked to see my mam there with my three sisters and brother. But my shock turned to something else when, after looking at my Mam's bruised face and black eye, I saw that my grandma also had a bruised face and a black eye and her arm was in a sling. They were both crying, telling me that Mam had left *him* again, but even worse, he'd burst into my grandma's house, hit Mam again and had then punched my grandma, knocking her over a chair and dislocating her elbow, for standing up to him.

I didn't know I was capable of such rage. My mind was racing with white-hot anger as I stood looking at my forlorn and distraught family and my hatred for my dad just boiled over. I didn't even stop to speak to anyone. I ran out of the house, jumped in my three-wheeler and set off to his house. My rage never left me. It was fuelled further as I thought of all the evil and violent things he'd done to my Mam over the years; how I'd felt belittled and disgusted by his behaviour. Now that he'd hit my grandma I was going to destroy him.

I ran into the house screaming and swearing at him to get outside and saying I was going to beat him to death. He was lying on the settee when I found him, but his position didn't reduce my boiling temper. I shouted that I would smash him to pieces where he lay or he could come outside and fight like a man and not like a coward. I was beyond control as I ranted to him about what he had done to my grandma and said he was going to pay for it.

As he followed me through the kitchen I saw the carving knife laying in the Lurpak butter on the table. I picked the knife up and threw it in the sink away from his reach. As he walked behind me he asked if I thought he would stab me in the back. I told him to bring it if he wanted and went down the path and stood in the road and waited for him. My engine was still running and the driver's door was open. He came out smirking and started to circle around me in a boxing pose.

After a few seconds of staring at his face I was simply

incandescent. I dropped my hands walked up to him and kicked as hard as I could in his balls. I hadn't planned to do that. I didn't have any strategy. I had no room inside my mind, it was too full of revenge for what he had done to my Mam all those years and finally what he'd done to my grandma. I had no control over my actions. I wanted to hurt him badly, humiliate him and break him as a man.

After he'd fallen to the ground I noticed quite a few of the neighbours were at their garden gates watching. The next-door neighbour shouted at me to let the police deal with him and at the same time police cars were suddenly screeching to a halt by the side of us. I was grabbed from behind, but I wasn't finished and struggled with them to get free to finish him off.

Then my original friendly police mentor appeared, thrusting his face in front of mine and telling me to calm down or I would lose my job. I was frantic and shouting that he'd beaten my grandma, but he did calm me down. As an officer picked my dad up he was still gasping and telling the police that no son of his would fight by kicking like that. I was shattered. The last thing I wanted to hear from him was to be called his son, and particularly someone like him quoting the Queensberry Rules.

I asked the policemen to let me go, saying I was calm and could be trusted. I walked to face my dad and told him to tell the police where the Lurpak butter came from. I turned to my friendly policeman and told him to call for CID to search the house for all the fags, drinks and food that were in it from the burglaries he'd carried out at the local shops and the Co-op. My dad went ashen and shouted to the neighbours that he was being turned in by his own son. What I said still embarrasses me, and I'm not proud of it, but I had to get rid of him, get him out of my life before I went too far. I knew instinctively that this was my opportunity to give my mother freedom. I would have preferred to have bashed his brains in. It was another of those moments when I made a potentially reckless decision on the spur of the moment, but it had the right outcome eventually.

Having said that, I found out much later that my Mam was not happy with my actions, although she never told me herself. In fact what I had done was never discussed, but my Mam and my siblings left that home in Holmgate to move to Clay Cross while he was in prison. My desire for revenge progressively diminished as I realised my family didn't appreciate my actions. Even my Uncle Gordon told me I shouldn't have turned him in. I still felt, though, that I had prevented a death that was surely going to happen. I always thought it would be Mam's at his hands, but when I look back at my uncontrolled rage when I faced him, it could quite easily have been his at mine. I've never felt like that since, although I subsequently knocked a few criminals out during violent arrests.

He was remanded in custody and stayed there until he went to prison, where he stayed for a couple of years. My Mam had some respite, but she believed I was wrong to turn him in. Even my grandma told me I shouldn't have done it, but she could understand why I was so angry. I didn't console myself by trying to justify my actions. If I hadn't seen the knife in the Lurpak in the kitchen it would never have occurred to me tell the police about his criminal behaviour. But I did console myself that my Mam and grandma had time ahead of them without having to worry about being beaten.

I returned home a couple of evenings during each of the next few weeks to give some support, but my Mam was a bit distant with me. As it became clear he was out of her hair for the considerable future, she started to relax and I saw some improvement in her attitude towards me and her own life in general. She told me she was excited about the council finding her another house a few miles away.

I never did ask or find out who contacted the police. They were at the house only moments after my arrival, so it's only now as I write this that I see that my Mam must have gone to the local phone box after I set off, knowing what my intentions were. There's no doubt that was the best thing that could have happened.

I was in trouble of course, and I expected the worst when I was told to report to the Chief Inspector of Cadets. My criminal behaviour could not be ignored by my superiors. He gave me a massive dressing down and telling off. He went on for ages about bringing the police service into disrepute, how I was so close to ruining my own career and life. He told me that I'd jeopardised all I'd achieved for one night of retribution. His was a great speech and I was not just frightened but humbled when he pointed out all the people I'd let down. He reminded me of all the people who'd shown such faith in me and those who'd helped me get to where I was, and not just the police.

He told me I was on the brink of becoming a police constable, that I was highly regarded and was expected to do well in the future and asked me if I would be capable of controlling my temper in the future. When it was my turn to speak I told him this was the first time I'd lost my temper (if you don't include my actions after being punched on the nose in the boxing ring as a kid) and it wouldn't ever happen again. I told him I was sorry about bringing the police service into disrepute and I hadn't considered the consequences of what I did. I told him that I wished my dad was dead. I asked him if I was being sacked. I looked straight at him when I asked him this question and I'm not sure if I was being belligerent or scared to death, but I wanted to know there and then.

He asked me to sit down at his desk and we talked for a long time about my family and my relationship with my grandma. He asked what I thought I wanted to do with my future. I remember telling him I wasn't a planner, I just wanted to be a policeman and to be good at my job. I left his office a very relieved young man, but with his warning about no more mistakes ringing very loudly in my ears.

I went back to work and nothing was ever mentioned by any officer, although I was expecting it, and I felt uncomfortable sometimes in their presence. I felt as if they knew but had decided not to bring it up. Thank you. I told Mrs Meredith everything of course.

A couple of months later, as Christmas approached, Mrs Meredith asked me to bring my mam to meet her for a little chat. I was surprised that my mam agreed. When I introduced them to each other, Mrs Meredith told me to come back in a couple of hours. On the way back with my mam, to her new council house in Clay Cross, she told me she'd had a good talk with Mrs Meredith and she thought she was a wonderful woman. She told me Mrs Meredith spoke highly of me. My mam told me that the two large boxes I'd put in the back of my car were full of joints of meat, eggs and vegetables and chocolates for the kids, a present from the Merediths. My mam told me that Mrs Meredith had also tried to give her some money, but she'd refused to accept it.

31

MAM'S DIVORCE, AND THE END OF MY STUTTER

The next time I saw my dad was just before I joined the regular police. My Mam asked me if I would attend Chesterfield Civil Court to help her with her divorce application. My dad was contesting it, and her solicitor had asked if I would give evidence to support her allegation of cruelty. How could he *ever* deny that? I said I would be delighted to give evidence against him. Because the court in Chesterfield was within my police force's boundary I felt I could travel there with a coat over my uniform and then take it off before getting into the witness box.

When I saw my mam outside the courtroom talking to the solicitor, I was staggered. She looked so small and frail. She was obviously afraid and nervous, not only of going into the courtroom, but having to face him again. I told the solicitor that there would be no need to ask my mam to speak in court. I told him I had all the evidence that was needed in my memory and it would justify the divorce.

It might sound a bit dramatic, but when my name was called I took my coat off to expose my uniform, stood in the witness box and stared across at him. I was going to beat him again. When I was given the Holy Bible and asked to repeat what was about to be said, I looked at the bench and said that I already knew the words. I stared at him as I said, without stuttering once, 'I swear by Almighty God that the evidence I shall give shall be the truth, the whole truth and nothing but the truth'. I was brought down to earth a little bit by the Chairman of the bench when he told me that in a civil court the witness only needs to promise to tell the truth, but that my oath would be more than enough. I wasn't swayed. I was totally focused and answered my mam's solicitor's questions clearly and accurately. I saw my mam crying as I related some of the horror stories and I was halted after about half an hour, in the middle of one account, when my dad's solicitor stood up and asked me to stop. He told the bench that his client's contention was withdrawn.

There was honour in it for me, and a massive relief that my Mam and siblings would have a future without fear of violence and that they would have enough money to go to the shop to buy food. My revulsion for him stayed the same. I had one last look at him as I stepped out of the witness box, but he kept his gaze down, and that was the last I ever saw of him.

I shared my experience with Mrs Meredith, and she helped me come to terms with my last contact with him. She agreed it was the best thing that could have happened for my mother and family. I told her I sometimes felt selfish for living my life and enjoying it so much when my family and particularly my Mam had it so hard. Cue more hugs, but a good talking to about making something of my life.

We also talked a lot about my forthcoming departure. I would be training at Pannal Ash near Harrogate for three months and would then be posted somewhere in Derbyshire. I had been told by my colleagues that it would not be Belper. We had a few sniffles as I tried to thank her for what she and her family had done for me, but, typically, I was really excited about the next massive change that was about to happen in my life. She laughed and told me it was not too late to become a nurse! I told her I would make her proud of me, but as a police officer.

My departure was quite low-key. My Bond had broken down a few weeks earlier and I couldn't afford to repair it, so I was given a lift to my grandma's by one of my constable colleagues. Handshakes and best wishes really. That's how the police force works; best friends one minute and ex-colleagues the next. It's the future that counts.

My time with Mrs Meredith was crucial. If I could change the world – and that was my intention at this stage of my life – I would have a Mrs Meredith in charge of every department in every company everywhere. And how many times did I go back and see her? You've guessed it. Manners and etiquette were still on my to-do list, but only after I'd overcome my next obstacle.

32

A POLICE CONSTABLE, A NEW CAREER, A NEW LIFE AND A NEW WIFE

▀▜▀▜▀▜▀▜▀▜▀▜▀▜▀▜▀▜▀▜▀▀

Thursday 4th September 1969 was my nineteenth birthday. The following Sunday I was dropped by a friend of my grandma's at Pannal Ash Police Training School near Harrogate in North Yorkshire, ready to start my three-month spell of training to become a police constable. I had to be ready to start at nine o'clock sharp the next morning. With my suitcase in one hand and my joining instructions in the other, I was marched to my four-bed dormitory room, then to my classroom and then to the dining room for my evening meal. I was told not to leave the grounds and, whatever I did, I was not to be late in the classroom the next day. Other than that the evening was mine. I was joined later by three new police officers, two from Nottingham Constabulary and one from Leicester Constabulary. We shared our excitement, our fears and trepidation, our ups and downs, in that dormitory room for the next three months.

I was in the classroom at eight o'clock, where I found the desk with my name plate on it and waited. Ten minutes later I fell in love with the next person who came through the door. She looked like Petula Clark in a policewoman's uniform. She was beautiful. She smiled cheerfully at me, her face enhanced by her dimples, and wished me good morning, very confidently. I know I was the only person there, but my heart and mind were doing somersaults, so I nodded back. Sheila Masters, soon to be known as Sheila Clements.

The three months' training were full of learning, excitement and tension. It truly was an intense training course. We learnt legal definitions parrot fashion and then learned what they meant and how to implement them, based on case law and our own role play. We studied every evening and I was often the last to leave the library, near midnight, especially if my future wife was studying with me. In the first month she didn't know she was going to be my wife of course. In fact she didn't even know I would be going out with her in the first month. But the time we spent together studying and walking the grounds together asking each other questions on what we'd learned drew us together emotionally.

The classwork was broken up by being trained to march in formation by a sergeant in a peaked cap whose screaming voice could be heard for miles, and his spittle had to be avoided from six feet away. We had to do cross-country runs, swimming and gym work. Sheila told me she fell in love with my legs when I was on the parallel bars before she fell in love with me as a person. But love it was. I scoured the shops and found a proper present for her 20th birthday in the October during our course. I wrapped it up and wrote something decent in the birthday card. Decent for me anyway!

I was however really saddened when I received a package through the post delivered to the training school. I opened it in front of Sheila and it was a presentation box containing a beautiful set of silver cuff links, from New Zealand, with a note from Nancy wishing me a happy birthday. I was elated and embarrassed at the same time. I reverted back to my normal rude and ignorant self and decided that sending a thank you note back to Nancy would undermine my new-found love for Sheila. So I did nothing, and I've regretted it to this day, even forty-odd years on. I should have been gracious and showed some manners, then, any time afterwards, and even now. My excuse is I haven't known her address in New Zealand since I finished my training. How pathetic. She was very special to me for a period in my life and I hope she has, and has had, someone very special throughout her life in New Zealand. I loved you, Nancy.

Sheila and I shared the same determination to succeed and win. She was very intelligent, having qualified as a State Registered Nurse, but had given that up to become a police officer. Of course, knowing what nurses get up to on duty did not influence my attraction and later love for her! At the end of the course, after the examinations had been completed, it was announced that Sheila had come top of our intake and I had come second – out of sixty constables. I'd found my true vocation in life – and a future wife.

I proposed to her before the final exams and wrote a letter to my Mam and grandma to tell them I would be getting married to a policewoman I'd met at training school.

Did I plan any of this? I proposed on the spur of the moment and wrote my letter home during a lecture that day, then borrowed a fellow constable's car and took Sheila home to witness me asking her dad's permission to marry her. We'd known each other for less than three months.

Sheila was allocated to a police station in Keighley in Yorkshire and I was stationed at Buxton in Derbyshire; only about fifty miles away as the crow flies, but no major road through the Peak District and with some of the Pennines in the way. But love overcomes everything. I lost count of the number of times I spent my days off hitch hiking from Buxton to Keighley and back again during the night, or to where her parents lived in a posh suburb of Leeds.

The first trip I made surprised both of us. I eventually arrived at her digs after a twelve-hour journey and knocked on the door. Sheila's landlady called her down from upstairs and we stood facing each other over the doorstep, both crying. She had in her hand the letter I'd posted two days earlier, which had just arrived, and she was only halfway through it. No mention in it of my cross-country hitch-hiking attempt. It was a spur of the moment decision.

Sheila visited me once and we went to Matlock, so I could show her where my career began, and onto Matlock Bath near to where the Trogs lived in the famous caves on the hillside. This was the Mods and Rockers era and Trogs were young, peaceful Jesus look-a-like vagrants who chose to live the simple humble life in the caves. I also heard them called 'cannabis smoking drop-outs' but I never spoke to any of them, seeing them only from a distance. They were harmless and not on my radar.

The hills and views were fantastic but not very romantic. In broad daylight we had a bash at making love, or rather had sex for a few seconds, for the first time, on the hillside, not far from the caves. It was not very satisfactory; it was hurried and furtive, and damp bordering on muddy, but we didn't care. It was exciting, and we were heading in the right direction. The kissing was great. And my determination to carry a clean handkerchief came in handy again.

My only recollection of note during my time at sleepy, boring Buxton Police Station was being called back to the station by the office sergeant in the early hours of one morning. I entered through the main entrance and before I entered the code to go to the private side I looked across the counter, where I could see into the office. The Office Sergeant was sitting talking to the Divisional Dog Handler. I only recognised him as a dog handler because of the massive German Shepherd next to him, staring at me and snarling viciously. Before I had time to start the code on the door, the handler shouted a word and his dog leapt into the air and was about to land on the counter in front of me. I could only stand frozen to the spot and stare at his massive head and mane of wild hair, his snarling teeth and wide eyes and hear the growling before, in the same breath as the first command, the handler gave another one-word shout. It was as if the dog had been shot. He landed on the counter, slid across it, dropped onto the floor at the side of me and lay there growling like a pack of dogs, with his teeth still snarling and just waiting to bite part of me off.

Meanwhile I stood rooted with one finger on the code box, petrified. My two colleagues thought it was hilarious. But that wasn't the reason I resigned from Derby County & Borough Police.

33

GOODBYE DERBY, HELLO LEEDS

Within a couple of months of being posted to Buxton, at a writing desk in the bedroom of my new digs, I wrote to the Chief Constable of Leeds City Police, unbeknown to anyone, and asked if they would consider transferring me to them from Derby County and Borough Police. I'd looked on a map and checked a police almanac at my police station for the address and knew the Leeds geographical area included my future in-laws' home and was not too far from Keighley in North Riding, where Sheila had been posted.

I received a reply some weeks later inviting me for an informal interview. I hitchhiked there of course and had no problems getting lifts as I was wearing my best, and only, suit, for the journey and interview. During the interview they advised me that Derbyshire Police would not consider wasting all the money they had spent on my cadetship and training school by allowing me to transfer to Leeds so early in my career and therefore nothing could proceed further. I asked the recruitment officer if they would accept me if I resigned from Derbyshire Police, as that seemed the obvious thing to do under the circumstances. He told me he couldn't give me that advice and I would be taking a risk because there were no vacancies in Leeds City Police at that time. He did tell me though that I would be a considerable asset to Leeds City Police if I did eventually join them.

I returned to Buxton and did my usual thing: I made a decision on the spur of the moment without considering the consequences. After being at Buxton for only three months, I wrote my notice out. It seemed all hell broke loose, and I was instructed to go our Headquarters in Alfreton, where I was interviewed by two police superintendents and a chief inspector. I was reminded in no uncertain terms what the Force had done for me over the years and advised that I had a great future with them. But I knew what I wanted and confirmed my resignation in the politest manner I could. It didn't go down very well. My new landlady wasn't very pleased either, but she wished me well.

As I worked my notice, I wrote to Leeds Police and told them I wanted to join them as an ex-Derby County and Borough Police Officer. After another visit to them, shortly afterwards, I was accepted and they provided me with some more digs with another landlady. I was within just two bus rides of my beloved in Keighley and one bus ride to her parents' home. I didn't own a car, as my three-wheeler love box was in Mrs Meredith's farmyard awaiting collection by a scrap dealer. I could not foresee buying a car on my meagre salary, but to our great surprise, Sheila's dad bought us one as a wedding present, a 1959 Austin A35. He was probably a bit fed up with me borrowing his company car at the drop of a hat.

How life changing was this move? I'd moved from a quiet rural county where my night duties consisted of checking that front and back doors of shops were secure to the drama and trauma of a very busy city where everything seemed to be done at a hundred miles an hour. Sheila was not too taken with police work at the sharp end, so she resigned and went to work at Leeds University as a librarian and returned to live with her parents. I should have picked up on this trait earlier; great in the classroom, but work-shy in the real world where you get paid for what you do. But love is blind.

I was in my element. I'd been posted to a police station called Ireland Wood, a suburb of Leeds City a couple of miles from where Sheila's parents lived. I found out on my first night that the reason there were vacancies was that four officers from my shift had been arrested and charged with theft. They'd attended a burglary at a shop in a rough, crime-riddled area and filled their panda car boots with goodies from the shop. All this whilst waiting for the scenes of crime officer to attend. A witness had watched their criminal behaviour through her bedroom window and reported it. The stolen property was recovered from the boots of their own cars that same night. So although there were no vacancies at the time of my first interview to join Leeds City Police, there was now a shortage of constables at Ireland Wood. So, without considering the consequences of resigning from the police in Derbyshire, despite being told there were no vacancies at that time in Leeds City Police, I did it anyway and a door conveniently opened, courtesy of some bent coppers! Or did those senior officers in Leeds City Police choose to have me because I was an asset?

Despite my relentless enthusiasm and naïveté I was given a dose of reality. I was working in a city where every policeman on my shift took it as a personal insult if he found there had been a burglary or car theft in the area he had been working during his previous shift. I soon started to share their determination and desire to capture criminals. The majority of us shared the ambition to become detectives. We ridiculed a couple of officers on our shift who had ambitions to join the traffic department by advising them that they would have to have to have a frontal lobotomy done first. There were some fantastic characters, with great camaraderie and an unshakeable belief in each other. Most of the officers on our shift were young, fit and dare I say, good looking, with a devil-may-care attitude. And all men. Policewomen had their own department and rank structure and didn't work nights in those days. The start of every shift generated excitement and bravado and bets on who would be first back at the nick with a prisoner.

34

DARK NIGHTING

On my second set of nights, just over a month after joining, I was fascinated to see two of our older officers, in their thirties, talking rather conspiratorially to a couple of detectives in a corner of the parade room. They were big rugby types, no-nonsense men who I had not exchanged words with. We had one rugby-playing bobby who was massive, but fast on his feet – and with his fists – despite his heavy drinking and smoking. He was pleasant enough, but always called me 'love'. I didn't like this and told him one day in no uncertain terms that if he kept calling me love, I'd invite him outside to sort it out. He walked past me into the parade room and told everyone, laughingly, that I was going to fight him if he didn't stop calling me love. He turned round and grabbed my lapels and pulled my face up to his and shouted, 'stop calling me 'duck' then!' We became good friends.

But going back to the two frightening characters who were talking to the two detectives. It was just after we'd started our night shift, and I watched as the officers took their uniform jackets off and turned them inside out. Then they put balaclavas on and went out with the other two, got into a CID car and drove off. They didn't even stay for the parade, but time was of the essence, apparently, as the pubs in those days closed at half past ten. I wouldn't have fancied bumping into those two at a wedding, never mind when they looked seriously like overweight SAS operatives. I asked a mate what was going on and he took me to one side and with great relish, but quietly, told me they were going 'dark nighting'.

In the early seventies there were a lot of property repair con men living in a rough area of Leeds, but on our patch. They were responsible for many burglaries where they duped elderly people into letting them into their houses on the pretence of making repairs. Often they stole money and jewellery without the elderly occupants knowing they'd done it, but sometimes they gratuitously assaulted them, and sometimes tied them up and threatened them with violence to give up their valuable possessions. The victims were always old and vulnerable and the events had a catastrophic effect on their lives and their relatives. These 'property repair' gangs were scum. They brazenly boasted of their crimes and were happy to show off in their groups and buy drinks for their mates in two particularly rough pubs in our area.

Detectives had difficulty proving any offences against these criminals because the witnesses were too old to make good identification, so they knew they were virtually invincible. And that's how the 'dark nighting' came about. The detectives knew these criminals and where they lived, which pubs they frequented and their routes home. The burly masked avengers, dressed suitably in black and not a shiny button in sight, each had a two-foot long three-by-two piece of wood and waited in a dark alley, in radio contact with the CID officers parked nearby, providing details of their journeys. As the scumbags walked round a corner their faces were met with a swinging piece of three by two, wielded by the dark nighters. I can't in honesty say it was justice, because I'd given the Queen's Oath, but it was definitely common-law retribution and I felt excited by what they were doing. It was never discussed by anyone, yet it seemed that the whole police station knew about it. These two were held in great awe by us mere mortals. Whenever we saw them in the pub after a shift, these vigilantes would always sit with the CID and never fraternise with us junior bobbies. Don't forget, this was still the very early 1970s.

I was encouraged by my new best friends to take part in some practical policing myself in my early days in Leeds City, and it stood me in good stead in the many years and incidents to come. I was taught to stand next to the ringleader of a gang or a group hell-bent on causing fights and disorder at the turning out of pubs and clubs on Fridays and Saturdays. I would spend time first identifying the leader of the pack, then work my way through the crowd until I was standing next to him. There's always one who can, with a bit of practice, be identified as the ringleader. He's usually not at the front where his minions are starting to threaten and disturb, but somewhere near the back, with a good view so he can orchestrate the mayhem. A similar practice adopted by police inspectors, or above, in violent situations; an ironic piece of symmetry, I eventually realised.

When I was certain I had the main man, I would make it known to the whole crowd, and particularly his followers, that I had identified him, and then look him straight in the eye and in a loud voice, say, 'Excuse me, you're standing where I want to stand.' After he's reluctantly moved a pace away, repeat the comment, again in a voice a bit quieter, but more menacingly. You quickly become the focal point of the crowd. The ringleader usually makes an effort to stand his ground and be a bit manly, but he knows that if he becomes abusive, or in any way violent, he's going to be the first one arrested and placed in a nearby police car or van. He has to make the choice of fight or flight. Will it be a rigorous arrest, or will he live to arrange a fight another day? If you get in early enough, and confidently enough, they usually choose the latter and their mates follow his example. But it was always a particularly exciting moment, waiting for him to decide. Fight or flight? Will I be fighting or smiling? It didn't always work of course, but we all took our knocks and bruises as part of the job and we always smiled after an arrest. I found that method of policing particularly exciting and effective. And often there was a bit of hero worship from adoring mini-clad ladies waiting for taxis after the excitement had died down.

I was as fit as anyone could be. I was doing life-saving training a couple of days or nights a week and I was captain of the Force's life-saving team. We competed in swimming as well as life-saving events around the country. I had even been taught to play tennis by Sheila's parents and played with them on my weekends off. They loaned me a racket – a wooden one with a sprung frame to prevent the head from warping when not in use – and I quickly became quite proficient. I spent a whole half day visiting sports shops in Leeds centre before buying a state- of-the-art fibreglass one made by Head. The only other time I'd experienced this euphoria was buying my red swimming trunks.

I was soon looking for players to give me a better game and even joined a local tennis club, only to find they were chalk to my cheese. But Sheila's parents didn't finish there. They taught me how to play Bridge and I was often on standby to fill in if one of the players couldn't make one of the regular Bridge nights at their house. I never told my grandma that I was a Bridge player – she would have thought that was too far-fetched. What a middle-class life! Where would I have been if it hadn't been Sheila first into our classroom at Pannal Ash Training School that day?

35

SEXUAL FREEDOM – AND A MORTGAGE

■▼■▼■▼■▼■▼■▼■▼■▼■▼■▼■

I could now see my beloved every day, depending on my shifts, although some of my new colleagues' company was so exciting I spent many hours working overtime with them. Our overtime was given freely and regularly. We weren't paid or given time off in lieu in those days, we did it for the joy of learning, the anticipation of catching criminals and the satisfaction and reward of great camaraderie.

However the frequent public meetings and clandestine trysts between Sheila and me created a lot of sexual tension between us. We met most days or nights at her parents' house. If I stayed at her house we had separate bedrooms of course, but we stole precious minutes to kiss and grope when out of sight of her family. Her mum or dad would always make plenty of noise coming back downstairs for a glass of water before we made too much progress.

Within a month I had left my latest landlady's lodgings and moved into a tiny bedsit on the ground floor of an old house near my police station. There was no love or loyalty in those lodgings; it was a job only for her and for many others housing young police officers in the area. My new place, all mine, had a shared bathroom and kitchen, but it was fantastic to be in my own place. How proud and independent did it make me feel?

Sheila and I agreed we would make love on my single bed the first night I moved in. My working day was full of sexual anticipation. I cleaned my room, the first time I had ever done any cleaning, to make sure the evening would be a success. I bought a bottle of German white wine and had a glass before Sheila arrived. What could go wrong?

We started kissing and fumbling as soon as she walked through my door, and I soon knew what would go wrong. I told Sheila that I needed the bathroom but then had to wait in the hallway outside the toilet until a flatmate got out of the bath. My erection was almost splitting the seams of my trousers. I didn't even lock the bathroom door. I masturbated as soon as I walked in and ejaculated all over the place within seconds. There was no toilet paper. I realised you had to bring your own. I used the curtains to wipe my willy, telling myself I would clean the bathroom the next morning so I didn't feel guilty. I went back to my room and started again, more confident now that our first performance on a bed would be memorable, or at least last a bit longer. It did, and it was.

It wasn't just a feeling of relief and achievement, it was love. Sheila told me she was a virgin and kept asking me if there was blood on the bed. That made it last a bit longer, but didn't dent my pride or enthusiasm or concern. There wasn't any blood and she explained that horse riding was known to break a girl's hymen sometimes and that she used to ride horses a lot. And I used a condom. I'd bought loads of them a few days earlier and put them in a drawer. If Sheila had found them I'm sure she would have thought she was going to marry a sex maniac. But in any case I fell asleep, happy and contented, straight afterwards.

Sheila added to my learning curve later by explaining that my behaviour by falling asleep was bad manners and I had some social graces to learn. She said she would teach me some skills I needed and that I would be a better police officer for it. She talked about English Literature and English Language and told me she would help my career. All this and we'd only made love once — or one and a half times, I suppose. I had other skills I wanted to hone, now I was awake. But I also agreed with her that I did need some coaching and it was a small price to pay.

She also told me, a year or so later, during an argument, that she'd actually lost her virginity when she was eighteen to a man ten years older than her, on the back seat of his Hillman Imp. She must have been a bit smaller then, I thought. Social graces and double standards came to mind! We were still in love at that particular juncture however, despite the arguments that had started to develop but, still, it didn't bode well for the future.

Within a few months of my joining Leeds City Police, Sheila and I had bought a semi-detached house on a lovely housing estate in quiet suburb called Cookridge – with a one hundred per cent mortgage. It should have been a ninety-five per cent mortgage, but it was organised through a colleague of mine who knew a solicitor who was not exactly scrupulous. It cost a fortune and everyone told me I was a fool to go into debt to the tune of £4,250. That house is worth about £300,000 now. Sheila and her mum were making marriage plans. We knew we would only live together once we were married.

We married in Sheila's local church. We were twenty years old. Mrs Meredith, my grandma and Mam came to our wedding, as did my sisters and brother. The reception was at Sheila's parents' house, because her dad had offered us the choice between a hotel wedding reception or a second-hand car.

Our honeymoon wasn't planned, so we set off in our four-wheeled wedding gift and ended up in Scarborough, after stopping at a garage half way there because the car was breaking down, or so we thought. The mechanic removed two large mackerel from the side of the engine, put there by jokers during the wedding reception. The fear of breaking down, and the smell, eventually disappeared. Our honeymoon of three nights consisted of making love, making love, making love and going the pictures in the town centre once to watch 'Love Story.' I was already missing work and my colleagues, so we set off to our new home in Cookridge, which had been duly decorated with balloons and garlands of 'Just Married' paraphernalia inside, outside and all over the house.

After all the determination, effort, risks and chances we had made and taken to be together, our marriage should have been idyllic, but that old saying 'marry in haste and repent at leisure' was already starting to apply.

I loved my job and wanted that sense of achievement, excitement and quality of working life to last forever. Consequently I spent more time at work, or associating with my colleagues, than I should have done. I realised a happy working life was not particularly conducive to a happy wife at home. We both wanted children, but it wasn't happening, though it wasn't through lack of trying. We were getting desperate and neither of us could quite come to terms with the fact that what should have been the most natural thing in the world was not happening to us. We didn't seek advice and perhaps we should have done. We had made friends with many of our neighbours, many of whom had small children. We were regularly asked by mothers and fathers when we were going to start a family – and by other husbands and wives if we wanted to go to their wife-swapping parties! The 70s were still swinging...

Sheila was still working as a librarian at Leeds University. Her qualifications seemed to get her a job anywhere she wanted. She did have a lot of certificates to prove her academic ability and to many people, with my lack of a single 'O' Level, we must have seemed like chalk and cheese - but it never crossed my mind at the time.

I didn't know it for a while, but one of our neighbours, Sheila's best friend and woman who spent many hours with her at our house or hers, or in night clubs, was sex mad. She was a part-time singer and entertainer and to describe her as vivacious would be a bit of an understatement. I suppose portraying her as a nymphomaniac might be an overstatement, but not by much. She was very attractive and knew it. Often when she and Sheila came back from clubbing, they would both come into the bedroom, wake me up and she would start to do a stripping act and ask if I wanted them both in bed with me. My answer was always the same, the second word being 'off'.

I warned Sheila that she was playing with fire knocking around with this friend, but I think her mate was her female alter-ego. Sheila was well-educated with a posh accent, a product of university-educated parents who were living in a four-bedroom detached house in a 'sought after area'. But

Sheila was not streetwise. She'd found someone else who was chalk to *her* cheese.

36

ANOTHER WIFE-BEATER

▛▞▞▞▞▞▞▞▞▞▞▞▞▞

I arrested many husbands over the years for beating or threatening their wives in drink, only for the wives to withdraw their statements the next day after their men were released on bail and had made their usual sober apologies and reminded them of their undying love. It didn't deter me and I never bore grudges. I always made myself available to women and families when I was asked to attend domestic disturbances, treating them with respect and determination to help them put their lives on a better footing.

While I was a young policeman at Ireland Wood Police Station, I was responsible for policing a rough estate where there was always fighting, assaults, burglaries and domestic disturbances on paydays from Friday through to Sunday. In the early hours of one night duty, after an anonymous 999 call about a disturbance, I attended a terraced house and was met by a woman whose face was so battered and bleeding she could hardly stand up. She was terrified of her husband, who had left the house when he had seen the blue light of my panda car. I told her not to worry and said I would lock him up when I found him and she would be safe.

A few minutes later the door opened and her husband appeared in the doorway – and completely filled it. He was massive and wearing a big heavy overcoat. I had about a 40-inch chest by now, but I was still very fit. He told me in a drunken Irish accent to get out of his house, with plenty of expletives mixed in. I put my helmet on, fastened the chinstrap and told him he was under arrest for assaulting his wife. I took hold of his lapels and pushed him back out of the house. He could easily have squashed me like a fly and I was vulnerable to any head butts and strikes from his fists, but I ducked his blows and kept repeating he was under arrest. He didn't manage to hit me and we walked backwards down the sloping street. He did succeed in knocking my helmet off, grabbing my personal radio off my lapel and throwing it away. He kept telling me to let go or he would beat me up, using many expletives in between, as he pushed and shoved. At times he was nearly falling on top of me and other times I was on my knees, but I never let go of him as we staggered down the street towards my panda car. I didn't have a plan, of course.

At the bottom of the street three panda cars came screaming round the corner and my colleagues jumped out and grabbed him. Someone in this rough area must have had a telephone and reported my predicament. My personal radio was lying in the road, smashed, and I hadn't had time to call for assistance.

He threw all of them to the ground and I was left still holding onto his lapels. Two more pandas arrived, including a very large sergeant who had served in South Africa and stood no nonsense from anyone. He told me to let go and he laid into the Irishman as the other officers re-grouped and jumped on his back. Eventually the Titan succumbed and allowed me to handcuff him. They just fitted his wrists.

I charged him with assaulting his wife (police officers took their knocks with good grace in those days, as long as the other person was in a worse state), and I released him on bail the following evening. I went to his house that night to check on his wife and take a statement of complaint. He was there, stone-cold sober, and greeted me like his best friend. Apologising to me, he told me I was stupid for trying to arrest him. What a charmer! He insisted we had a glass of Jameson's Irish whiskey to celebrate his love for his wife.

She withdrew her complaint of course, and no amount of warnings from me about teaching him a lesson could change her mind. I told him how lucky he was to have such a loving and devoted wife. I gave him a seriously strong warning, with plenty of expletives of my own, that he would be in prison faster than he could drink a glass of whiskey if he ever laid a finger on her again. I kept to my side of the bargain and called to their house at least weekly over the next few months to check on her physical appearance. All seemed well.

All the neighbours knew how he treated his long-suffering wife, but importantly they knew they could rely on me to do something about it. I became a bit of a celebrity in their area and was never short of invitations into houses for cups of tea, especially the Irish families. Whenever I saw my wife-beating Irishman, or him and his wife, in the street when I was working in their area they would wave or stop for a chat like life-long friends. It was a very rewarding episode for me, because I also learned that arresting a wife-beater and taking him to court and prison was not always the best course of action. Although I'm convinced she would have been much better off without him, during my time working in that area there were no more issues. I can't help but think, with a little bitterness, that somebody ought to have got to my dad in the same way, before it became a habit for him and a way of life for my mam.

I always sided with the woman in these scenarios when I saw them bruised and battered. I enjoyed arresting their men, and woe betide any who showed any resistance. I wanted them to know what it felt like, whenever I was given the opportunity. Although I arrested many, and even got as far as the courtroom with some, in those days the women always gave in and eventually withdrew their complaints. Such was the 1970s. It never deterred me, but I was obviously ahead of my time. These offences are taken much more seriously nowadays, and women and their children are better off for it.

But 'the Job,' as police officers refer to it, was taking me over. I was addicted to the excitement of locking up criminals. For me it was this simple: how dare men, and sometimes women, think it's okay to break into someone's house and steal their personal property? What gave them the right to cause wanton damage, steal, sell drugs, or attack people with mindless violence, or rule, control or rape women? I was having no excuses, and it seemed sometimes like a personal crusade. Even off duty I would stop fights and throw fighters off buses, and all this in front of my wife, who did not share my passion for upholding the law.

One incident in particular comes to mind, and again if

I'd considered that I might have been putting my friends in danger, I might have thought twice. But probably not. I was on my way to Dublin for a weekend with three good friends, not police officers, on the car ferry from North Wales when I visited the toilets. It was busy, with about eight urinals and sinks and queues for each. As I turned away from the stall I'd been using to the nearest washbasin the bloke who took my place lit up a cigarette. He was dressed in a lumberjack-type shirt, full head of hair and big beard, probably in his forties. A lot of the men turned and looked, because there were signs everywhere stating it was a no smoking area. He left the cigarette in his mouth and totally ignored the young ferry attendant, who was in his company uniform, repeatedly telling him that smoking was not allowed in the toilets. The lad even told him he was allowed to smoke at the rear of the ferry, outside. The man ignored him completely.

Eventually he casually zipped himself up, long cigarette dangling from his lips, ignored the lad and walked to the wash basin next to me. A lot of the men left the area, to find another toilet, presumably because of embarrassment. The ignorant smoker didn't even wash his hands, but stood in front of the mirror combing his hair. I'll give the uniformed employee his due; he stood behind him stubbornly repeating his mantra that it was a no smoking area.

I looked up from my basin, my taps still running, and decided to tell him to put his fag out. Then I noticed the smirk he had on his face, presumably because of the effect he was having on everyone. I'd seen that look in a mirror many times before – it was just the Brylcreem that was missing.

That's when my brain went missing, and in less than a second I scooped two hands and forearms of water from my bowl into his face from about two feet. The effect was immediate. His fag was not only extinguished, it was lost in his wet beard. As the startled look on his face turned to thunder, I had my left hand in his beard and my right fist about a foot from his face. My face was closer to him than his beard was and just as his fists started to rise I made a snarling comment about 'move any more and I'll smash your face in'. There might have been the F word in there too for good measure.

The men at the urinals and sinks started scrambling for the exit, but I wasn't thinking about them. Suddenly he spread his arms out and said in a very placatory manner, 'OK, OK, I'm not a violent man'. I released him straight away and he took the opportunity to join the queue at the exit door. I saw him pull the soggy fag out of his beard and throw it on the floor. I let that go. As I stood getting my breath back and turned my taps off, there was one old man with a walking stick still standing at one of the urinals who looked across and said, 'Good on yer lad!'

The ferry attendant was shaking and kept saying thank you, thank you. I told him he should be proud of himself for standing up to the bloke in the first place.

I went back to my mates and told the driver he could drink if he wanted to, as I would drive when we got to Dublin. I told him I wouldn't be drinking any more until we reached the hotel. I'd seen the soggy fagger standing with half a dozen of his mates across the bar watching us. I didn't tell my mates what had happened and hoped he wasn't going to share his humiliation with his group. All went well and I told my mates what had happened over a few pints that night. They weren't impressed, of course.

Even while in uniform patrolling the streets, I was renowned throughout Leeds City Police for having so many informants. Somehow I attracted criminals who wanted to grass up others. I've never been able to explain it, other than the fact that I treated everyone fairly (apart from wife beaters) and I always tried to help these people with their problems. I took a genuine interest in their welfare and would go out of my way to visit them and meet their families, or sit and talk and give advice. But these informants, or snouts as we called them in Leeds, were responsible for my one-man band of crime detection.

I came to the notice of the local CID officers, who would offer to buy me beer if I shared my info or let them join me in the many arrests I made, thanks to my grasses' regular source of information. I had become addicted to knocking doors down and applying handcuffs. Foolishly, I never considered my safety when I went on my own rampages, emerging with a suspect and later ensuring a court appearance, conviction and jail term. I even found I was good at preparing the files for the prosecution. Taking witness statements was easy, but putting together a summary involving numerous or complicated offences and defendants was considered an art. I often received congratulations from the police prosecutors for providing them with a readable and accurate summary of events that they could read out verbatim in court. It is thanks to Constable (later Chief Superintendent) Dave Higgins at Belper Police Station, who taught and trusted me to take witness statements, that I had this ability to show clarity, continuity and chronology in my court papers.

Our local solicitors (and later barristers in complicated drugs cases) enjoyed my company, and I theirs. I was in my element, and it was only a matter of time before I was invited to join a plain clothes department where my natural talents (not my own words, I would add modestly) could be better used. And eventually I did, joining Vice Squad, then Drug Squad and eventually the CID over the course of my career. But, as I found to mine and Sheila's cost, working in these departments is not conducive to a solid and happy marriage.

37

SEX IN THE SADDLE

▪▪▪▪▪▪▪▪▪▪▪▪▪▪▪▪

Now, going back a few pages, talking of horses and hymens... I hadn't been in Leeds City Police long when I was given a beat in the Headingley and Meanwood areas, on the outskirts of the city, to manage on foot patrol. One day, by chance and being inquisitive, I found myself down a secluded little lane where there was a riding school. You don't need to introduce yourself when in uniform, and it wasn't long before I was invited into the reception for a coffee. I watched all sorts of different shapes and sizes of people having lessons as I listened to the owner's complaints of vandalism and petty thefts by local youths. In return for a warm and pleasant welcome, to include tea and coffee on any visits to the stables in the future, I promised I would pay particular attention to the security and well-being of his premises when they were closed.

It hadn't taken me long to get to know the local trouble makers in Meanwood and encourage loose talk from small-time informants. I soon found out who the young villains were who were responsible for raiding the stables. I spoke to some of the gang in the streets and warned them off, then went to the main leader at his home and spoke to him in front of his parents, leaving them in no doubt that he and his parents would be spending more time at the police station with me if there was any more vandalism at the stables. It worked, and it stopped. And of course I was made even more welcome at the riding school.

I'd never been astride a horse in my life and for a bit of fun for all, I climbed on one large nag and paraded around the area for all to see – in my uniform. I became addicted and visited after work and paid for a couple of lessons. I'm sure I was getting double the time for my money and it only took a couple of weeks before I felt quite comfortable in the saddle. I was young and enthusiastic enough to only want to go fast; plodding around the local bridleways seemed quite boring.

I asked the manager if I could hire my favourite horse, Minstrel, for a week and it was arranged. I was living with my future in-laws at this time, in a posh suburb of Leeds called Bramhope. They had a big garden and in my enthusiastic innocence I assumed I could ride him the five miles to their house and leave him in the back garden and ride him every day during that week of my annual leave.

However, it took me over four hours to get there. Once we reached the point a couple of hundred yards down the road from the stables where Minstrel normally turned left onto a bridleway, he refused to go straight on. We went round in circles on his own axis as I pulled on the reins, left and right, until I eventually gave up, dismounted and led him by the bit past the turn off. As soon as I mounted he walked straight back to the turn off to his normal route. I ended up walking and pulling him away from there for half a mile until he was disorientated and I was furiously embarrassed. And then we were faced with the traffic lights at the main A660 — five lanes — crossroads in Headingley, the road between Leeds and Otley. We went to the centre of the road to turn right, then stood and watched as the lights turned from green to red a dozen or more times. Minstrel just stood still as cars went round us, in front and behind. To my eternal mortification I eventually dismounted and dragged him, by the bit, through the lights. Even during this manoeuvre the lights changed at least twice, and there were plenty of comments from motorists as they passed us. Most of them were funny. It could have been worse – I could have been in uniform.

There was a fantastic upside to all this. After tying Minstrel to the drainpipe at the front of my in-laws' house I went in, knackered, to make some lunch. I was followed in almost immediately by my mother-in-law, who was shouting in astonishment that someone had tied a horse to the drainpipe at the front of the house. She was a good sport though. After refusing my request to house Minstrel in their back garden, she telephoned a farmer friend who she knew had some fields nearby. She went off to borrow a key for the lock on a gate to one of the fields and I met her there.

The next day, after failing to catch Minstrel and saddle him, I returned with a bucket of feed and enticed him to the gate. We went off for the day and whenever I found a gate to a field or wood open, we went off for a canter. And this is where it got very interesting. I met a fellow equestrian. She was a couple of years older than me, married, tall, blonde, beautiful and very posh, on a magnificent black horse. My

Clay Cross accent was still difficult to understand, as my fellow officers kept reminding me, but it was not a barrier here, because it transpired we had a lot in common. She loved riding and jumping and had a thirst for excitement and an insatiable desire for sex. Outdoors though!

A couple of months after I'd ridden a now very well-behaved and fitter Minstrel back to his stables to renew his monotonous daily plodding of the local circuit, I met the horse lady by chance and arranged to go riding with her. She had a spare horse she wanted exercising and asked me to meet her at her stables the next day. Free riding, and if the horse that needed exercise was anything like the one I'd seen her riding, I was in for a teat. Did I just say teat? I meant treat, but no matter. And I was in for a treat – greater than any imaginable. I'd never galloped with Minstrel. Sitting on his back was like sitting in an armchair, and after a couple of hundred yards of cantering he needed a five-minute rest. This horse needed no encouragement – in fact I was lucky to remain seated once we were in the fields and woods. We dashed along side by side laughing in the excitement of it all.

Later in the day I had a Robin Hood moment as we cantered through some woods. I leaned up, grabbed the branch of a tree and let the momentum swing me out of the saddle and up into the branches. She rescued my horse and as I dropped back into the saddle, I fell to the ground. She quickly jumped down and kissed me, and we ended up making love on the ground there and then. It was furious and fantastic. How did I end up here? My most exotic purchase prior to hiring Minstrel for a week had been those red swimming trunks. Exotic had become erotic, and my life had become so exciting.

We met at least weekly for riding and outdoor sex, but

the most memorable day was when she turned into Lady Godiva. She suggested we had sex on one of the horses. It was a secluded place – I hoped! Both naked, we tried with me sitting normally with my feet in the stirrups and her sitting astride me facing me. But as soon as we were positioned to start thrusting, the horse moved forward and one or both of us fell off. We persisted. We tried her in front of me, leaning onto the horse's neck and even me lying with my head on the horse's rump and her astride me. But every time we got to the serious part, the horse set off and we fell off. There was a great deal of laughter, but there was also a great deal of determination, followed by frustration, followed by giving up mounted sex and making good use of the soft ground.

She was out of my league though, and when the excitement and sexual intimacy started to wane so did the relationship. Yet I was still on my mission of exciting discovery and it seemed that wherever I looked, or turned, or opened a door, excitement beckoned, so I selfishly, but happily, moved onwards, taking my memories with me.

38

FROSTED GLASS

Sheila had by now resigned her librarian post as it was boring, and started nursing again, working part-time on nights at a cottage hospital near Leeds. I would invariably drop her off and pick her up the following morning. If I was working an early shift I or a colleague would pick her up from the hospital in a panda car and bring her home. Seven o' clock in the morning was usually a quiet time, but on this particular occasion, one of our shift sergeants saw me driving her home, obviously not on the beat area I had been allocated that morning. He chased me, but lost me. I was told by personal radio to return from wherever I was to the police station to explain who my passenger was.

I had no qualms in explaining what I had done, but was told by him that I was neglecting my duty. Of course I argued that everything I did was relevant and that what I had done took only minutes out of my work schedule, and that he and everyone at the police station and the whole community received far more from me than what I was paid to do.

It didn't wash, and after he had cleared it with the Superintendent, he told me in a cocky manner that I was being transferred to Millgarth Street, a famous old police station in Leeds city centre, as of the next day. I was outraged, and there was an outcry from all the police officers I worked with – including a number of CID detectives. All to no avail though and I reported to the Superintendent at Millgarth Street the next day, saluting smartly and telling him I would be a bonus to whatever team he put me with. He even said he knew of me and that I was welcome. What a great move it turned out to be.

I stayed in touch with my mates at Ireland Wood police station and not long after I'd moved I shared a great night out in the city centre with one of them. He dropped me off at the end of my street in the early hours. It was summer and just getting light and as I quietly closed his car door at the end of our street I heard a woman's voice say that I was going to get into trouble with Sheila coming home this late. It was Sheila's alter ego, leaning out of her bedroom window. Her husband worked abroad for months at a time and she was obviously on her own.

She told me I should have a coffee before I went home. Although I was only twenty yards from my front door, I accepted the offer. She was wearing one of those baby-doll negligees and quite obviously nothing else. Before I tasted the coffee we'd made frantic love all over her kitchen. She was wild and fun and obviously missing her husband. We had the coffee, then started making love on all the furniture in the front room. She was insatiable. I left her house at about six o'clock that morning as people were going to work and walked the thirty yards to my own house.

I was woken up a couple of hours later with a cup of tea from Sheila, who said was she was going the shops. The shops were just around the corner, a few hundred yards away. I came downstairs in a pair of shorts just as my sex-mad friend walked into our house through the back door. This wasn't unusual, but under the circumstances I thought she had a bit of a cheek. Neither of us was embarrassed and I told her that Sheila had just gone to the shops. She told me she had watched her set off and that she was frantic for more sex. I wasn't really up for this, and told her Sheila might catch us.

She held my hand and pulled me to the front door, where there was a frosted pane of glass next to the door above the window sill. She bent over with her face pushed up to the frosted glass and said she would watch for Sheila coming back. She lifted her short dress up, revealing that she was wearing no knickers, opened her legs and forced me to do the deed...

Timing is everything, as they say, and just as we finished, Sheila walked down the drive. I ran upstairs to the bathroom and my sex fiend went to greet Sheila and put the kettle on. They were drinking coffee and chatting away in the front room when I came down and told them I had to go to work early.

I've wondered since if it was my growing irresistible charm that attracted her or if I had been set up again. I suppose if I was completely two-faced I would say my sex fiend friend was a bad influence on my wife too. She insisted on taking Sheila out regularly to parties and for drinks with her friends. I'm sure some of her attitude rubbed off on

Sheila at that time. All this was before our children were born, thankfully.

Over the next year or two our friend called round to our house many times each week and if Sheila was watching television or in the bath she would insist on giving me a blow job in our kitchen. She was sex mad, funny and unfortunately, irresistible. She never wore knickers, at least in the summer, and sometimes when she visited our house she would stand behind Sheila and lift her dress up, baring all, to see if she could get a reaction from me as I stared past Sheila at her.

There has been a long-term legacy from this; I find it difficult to look through someone's frosted glass windows from inside their front doors without smiling, and I've made sure that none of the many houses I've bought or chosen to live in have ever had that temptation.

39

VICE AND THE VICE SQUAD

I'd been at Millgarth Street for about three years and was having a whale of a time. I'd been promoted into the local Vice Squad and found another niche in my vocation. My confidence was as high as it could be and I felt I could rule the world. I was mixing with a group of fellow officers, men and women who were all like-minded about the Job and I would socialize with them. I was drinking by now, socially, but never drunk. My life changed progressively, but in the wrong direction, when I found I could flirt quite easily, and often one thing led to another. I was soon having occasional short affairs, mainly with like-minded police women.

Before you get too disapproving, I should say that Sheila, having gone back to nursing, was also having affairs at work and was having great nights out with her friends locally. It was unspoken by either of us, but we both knew we could easily prove infidelity if we wanted to. We had been invited a few times to join in the partner swapping that went on in and around our street, but we were both more discreet and declined. Well, almost. My Leeds Vice Squad days were a learning curve, full of excitement, humour, unusual arrests, unusual sex (not involving me) and usual sex (involving me).

One memorable arrest from that time resulted in an appearance at Leeds Magistrates Court. One of our roles, as plain clothes officers, was to visit public toilets legally for corroboration purposes and to deter homosexuals and paedophiles from using the toilets for criminal purposes. Our reaction and response were based on complaints from parents that their sons had witnessed offensive sexual activities, or had been propositioned, in various public toilets in the city.

We worked in pairs and would always enter a public toilet separately and choose a urinal two or three stalls away from each other and watch what was going on. Usually nothing happened for a few minutes until the occupants believed you had overstayed the normal time to urinate and therefore might be one of them. On this occasion an elderly man stood next to me, caught my eye and turned to show me his erect penis, which he was stroking slowly. Bearing in mind I was in my early twenties, so a man who seemed old to me then might been in his fifties. Nevertheless I showed him my warrant card and arrested him for the offence of being 'Male Person Importuning for an Immoral Purpose' (Sexual Offences Act 1956). This was not an unusual occurrence, as working in pairs we regularly arrested half a dozen men in toilets for this or similar offences in one shift.

This man was different though. He cried all the way to

the police station. Although he agreed that what he'd done was wrong, he blamed his behaviour on the tablets he was taking since his wife had died six months earlier. He said it was his first time and he couldn't explain why he'd suddenly had the desire to play with another man's penis. I believed him. However he was still charged and bailed to attend our magistrates' court a few weeks later. I never gave it any thought until his court appearance.

In these cases the first officer in the case, usually the arresting officer, always attended court, even in guilty pleas. After the case, but before sentencing, it was the duty of this officer to go into the witness box and read out the defendant's antecedents and previous convictions, if applicable. This poor man had brought his son to court, and he was prepared to speak up on his dad's behalf if the court would let him. I spoke to him at length. He fully supported his dad and was hoping to reduce to a minimum whatever sentence the magistrates decided to impose. His dad fully intended to plead guilty in the hope of minimising any newspaper coverage (although he had actually travelled from Sheffield to Leeds to carry out his folly), so the chances of his friends getting to know were slim. There was of course an even slimmer chance of his dad being recognised by a neighbour from Sheffield in a Leeds public toilet!

I agreed with his son that I would speak up on his behalf and he was relieved that he wouldn't have the trauma of speaking from the witness box. So I hatched a plan, but kept it to myself. The prosecution read out my summary of the offence and his activities. He did not want to be represented, so there was no defence solicitor trying to make a name for himself and tout for business in front of the many criminals and their friends waiting in the gallery.

I entered the witness box and gave the oath, name and

rank. I read out his antecedents, said he had no previous convictions and then explained how supportive his family was and that there was no doubt in my mind that his unusual behaviour was somehow connected to losing his wife earlier and to the tablets he was taking. I could see the three magistrates nodding their heads and knew that they appreciated the support I was giving him. And then I said, 'As far as I'm concerned, Your Worships, I believe this was just a flash in the pan.'

I stood stock still and looked at the magistrates. The first one to crack was the clerk. She put her hand over her mouth and started shaking, but a high-pitched shriek came out and she stood up. The magistrates suddenly cottoned on and one of them let out a bellowing snort, followed by heartfelt laughter. They all stood up and together rushed out of the door of the court, into their chambers. Outside, their laughter increased in volume so I could clearly hear them, even though it was difficult because of the laughter coming from everyone in the public gallery.

After a few minutes the Magistrate's Clerk returned to her desk. Just as she started to ask all to stand, she made the mistake of looking at me. I stared back at her with only the slightest hint of a smile and as she said the word 'stand' her voice shrieked again, just as the magistrates were coming back in. She pushed into them in her haste to leave while they all had their hands over their mouths, I suppose trying to show some respect.

When they eventually took their seats, the court was quiet. I noticed that the Magistrate's Clerk had not returned. The Senior Magistrate, in a tightly-controlled voice, said, 'Thank you Officer,' and turned to the Defendant, the only person, other than me, who had not laughed out loud, and thanked him for his guilty plea. His and the other magistrates' shoulders were all shaking as he said in a querulous voice, that under the circumstances, a 'conditional discharge is most appropriate'. It was riotous, and the magistrates scrambled for the door. I discovered later that their caseload for the rest of the day was shared out amongst the other courts and the room locked. They were unfit for duty.

I was famous for weeks. Some months later I was invited to the magistrates' clerks' Christmas party so I could re-enact the whole episode in front of them all. It was light relief in what was a very exciting but, without question stressful, job. Although It had its perks too I suppose.

40

ARRESTING A MURDERER

Within a few weeks of becoming a Vice Squad officer, I arrested a man for murder. Unfortunately I was told by the night superintendent that because I hadn't quite followed the correct procedure it would be better all round if he was the arresting officer. He explained that it would be dealt with at Crown Court and I didn't have sufficient experience. I didn't know better at that time, and my obedience to such a high rank was absolute. But the circumstances of the arrest are worth mentioning. Peter Stringfellow's first night club, Cinderellas/Rockefellas, was in Leeds City centre, and as the club was closing one night a group of West Indians had a bit of an altercation with a group of local white youths outside the main door at the top of the steps. It ended up with one of the white youths being punched, falling down the stairs and dying. There were many altercations of this type in and around Leeds, so it wasn't unusual to hear that a group of youths were wanted for questioning about a murder. But no one was coming forward with information, no progress was being made and after a couple of months it had gone cold, although a team of detectives were still investigating it.

On this particular Saturday night, I was in a city centre pub when one of my many informants asked me if I was involved in the search for the bloke who had murdered the guy in the fight outside Stringfellows. After a few drinks he told me the Jamaican responsible was in a blacks-only night club in the basement of a building on the main street through the city, the Headrow. He gave me a perfect description of him and in particular his style and clothing and how his dreadlocks were fastened.

I knew of this club, but I also knew that as it wasn't licensed I, and any other police officer, would be very unwelcome. I had never visited it, although I regularly visited every licensed premises as part of my job. I didn't know the layout, only that it was in the basement – but you could hear the sound of Bob Marley being played from the opposite side of the road anyway. When I told my long-suffering, rather nervous sometimes, Vice Squad partner what I intended to do, he advised getting back-up from our uniform and CID colleagues first and doing a formal raid. I asked him to wait at the top of the steps and if there was trouble to radio for assistance. Our police station was less than a hundred yards away, so he could shout if need be. I was still on my learning curve about planning!

The bouncer on the door tried to stop me going in, but my warrant card and my enthusiasm eventually got me past him. The basement was packed, so my entrance went unnoticed and there was no point in asking any questions anyway because we would all have had to lip read or know sign language. I'd spotted my man as I walked down the stairs. He was in the middle of the dance floor and even though it was crowded, my informant's description of his clothes, hair and aggressive style of dancing was plain to see. All I had to do was push through the throng, arrest him and get back out.

The thing that gets me now, looking back, is that I had no fear that I might get into trouble or that my arrest attempt would fail. I had no hesitation whatsoever. I'm more nervous writing it now than I was when I locked him up. Thanks to the noise in the place, when I did get hold of him on the dance floor, he pulled away because he couldn't hear me telling him who I was, or that I was arresting him for murder. (The night Superintendent later picked up on this technicality, and that's how he came to be arresting officer on the subsequent paper work and not me!) However, it was plain to see, despite the darkness, and my warrant card briefly shown, that I was a police officer and that my confrontation with the dancer could only mean I was arresting him. He started Kung-Fu-type arm waving and kicking and the crowd opened up into a circle around us. Exactly at the moment the lights came on and music stopped I punched him hard in the face, grabbed his dreadlocks and started dragging him backwards through the circle of nightclub goers. Everyone must have been stunned, because the nearest ones parted to let us through, up the stairs and onto the road.

My colleague ran across the road to join us and together we calmly walked him into the police station. Ten minutes later there was a small noisy demonstration outside the police station as his mates and other night clubbers voiced their anger at my trespass— by which time I wasn't the arresting officer any more.

41

UGLY DUCKLING TO BEAUTIFUL SWAN

■▼■▼■▼■▼■▼■▼■▼■▼■▼■▼■

Not long into my time in this department and still in my early twenties, I became involved in a serious case of assault that had a very unexpected outcome.

As the on-duty vice squad officer, I was asked one day to visit Leeds General Infirmary (LGI) to investigate a serious assault on a woman. The ambulance had brought in a woman found in the street with facial and body injuries that appeared to be life-threatening. I only recognised her as female because of her clothes. Her face had almost been pulped and was so swollen it did not even look like a face. As the nurses took her clothes off her, her body too revealed massive bruising and swellings. She had been unconscious and was on a drip. She looked as though she had been in several car accidents rather than being assaulted, but the medical staff assured me her injuries were consistent with a savage physical assault.

My vigilante instincts were alerted. I typed up a report back at the Vice Squad office and recommended I continued with the investigation when I returned to work the next day. I visited her twice a day, until after almost a week she was able to tell me that her 'boyfriend' had been responsible. Not a term I would have used! I was outraged, as you can imagine, and could hardly wait to take her full statement before I went after him. It still took two days before I could take her statement. She could hardly speak, she was in agony but worst of all she was terrified of him, and towards the end of the statement she wanted to withdraw it. He'd hit her many times before, but she had not spoken to the police because of his threats of more violence if she did. She told me her sister, who lived nearby, and her own parents, who lived in Scotland, were just as frightened of him.

I was quietly incandescent with rage towards him, but calmly advised her that this time she had to go through with her complaint and I would be with her every step of the way. I repeatedly assured her that he would be in custody for a long time by the time I'd finished with him and that I would certainly have him in custody before she was released from hospital. She eventually agreed, a couple of weeks after she had been assaulted. The swellings of her face and head were only just beginning to reduce to the point where she was recognisable as a human being.

I arranged with her sister for the woman to live with her on release from hospital. I also helped move her personal things from her boyfriend's flat — after I'd arrested him. When I finally did arrest him it was such a pleasure. I know that might sound selfish to some, and it might be said I should have been more professional in my attitude and behaviour, but he belonged in captivity, caged with other wild animals. My colleague waited in the squad car outside the house where I found out he was hiding. As I dragged him to the car, I told my colleague that he had tried to escape when I arrested him.

By the time I interviewed him in the Bridewell, where the cells and interview rooms are below the Magistrates' Court and Crown Court in the city centre, he was malleable. I was fuelled by anger towards him and I knew he could tell that I was on the point of exploding as I took his statement. He admitted everything straight away and even asked me to apologise to his girlfriend for him. I told him in no uncertain terms that her memory of him was going to be erased and if he attempted to make contact with her from prison or on his release he would have me to deal with on a personal level. I meant every word I said, and said it with plenty of venom. He even told me that he knew prison was the only way to prevent him from losing his temper. He was a self-employed builder and plasterer and a drinker and, according to his ex-girlfriend, charming when sober.

I charged him with Section 18, grievous bodily harm, opposed his bail and he was remanded in custody until his trial at Crown Court. He pleaded guilty. His ex didn't attend court and it was months before she could relax and truly believe he was history. The judge said he found the photographs of the woman's injuries harrowing. He was sentenced to four years in prison. I delighted in visiting her and her sister and telling them the result.

By this time, unfortunately for my rocky marriage, Morag had turned from a very ugly duckling into a beautiful swan. We had bonded during the many hours we had spent together in hospital and at her sister's flat as I kept my promise to make her feel safe. We were totally at ease with one another. I'd kept my word, and she felt safe and happy for the first time in years. Her parents and sister thought I was wonderful and I was invited off duty out for meals and to socialise with them. There were no children in my marriage at this time, and not much else in it either. It's no excuse, but I seemed to be making up for the time I lost seeking to lose my virginity. I had married young and I was still young. I was living my life like a child in a sweet shop and doing a job I loved at a hundred miles an hour.

Because my swan and I had started our relationship in such a platonic way, with me as the protector, it was very comfortable to take the next step. Her sister started it by walking out of her own flat, telling us that she was going to the pictures and we should make love before she came back. It was as natural as that, and afterwards we went to the pub next door, where we later met her sister and thanked her for the advice. We had a very warm and sexually satisfying relationship for a number of months.

Our relationship came to an end through my own enforced inactivity. While decorating the sitting room at home, I collapsed unconscious and was rushed to hospital by ambulance. I had to have an emergency operation to remove my gangrenous appendix. The operation apparently just saved my life, as it was about to burst. When I was in the recovery room the attending nurse explained all the gory details and even showed me the offending appendix displayed in a jar. I'm sure some nurses think police patients don't have feelings.

I can give a great example here of how life in the NHS has changed from the early seventies to the 21st century — and no stitches or sex involved. I was sharing a room with three other men, all of whom were more mobile than I was. I had a visit from my best friend, a colleague with whom I'd shared hundreds of arrests and whom I would trust with my life. In fact, I was to become his best man, and he would be my best man at my second marriage when he made the worst faux pas any best man could make. He did a great job of making his humorous and serious best man speech in front of a hundred people – until his final sentence. He asked all to be upstanding and drink a toast 'to the bride and groom, Nick and Sheila'. I was actually marrying Lorraine. The response to the toast was normal, until most realised the mistake and their voices trailed off when they reached 'Sheila'. Tears were shed, a lot of them his, but it was memorable. Hope you're still out there, John. Haven't seen you since the wedding – over thirty years ago!

Anyway, John came to visit me in my hospital bed, and true to form he could be heard clanking down the corridor as the cans of beer he'd brought with him rattled in his pockets. Just as he was handing them over, the nursing Sister came in and saw what was happening. She shouted at John, letting him know in no uncertain terms that I was her patient and she would decide when and if I was allowed alcohol. She then physically threw him out of the ward along with the cans of beer and scolded the four of us in our beds like we were naughty children.

Fortunately we were on the ground floor. Half an hour later there was a knock at the window of our room. When one of the patients opened the curtains, there were four pints of Tetley's bitter standing on the window sill. So we duly behaved like men (or maybe naughty children) and drank a toast to the nasty Sister.

I had plenty of other visitors to the hospital, including, whilst still bedridden but at home, a visit to my front door by my beautiful swan. She'd made her own investigations to find out where I lived and was concerned about my sudden lack of visits to her little cottage. She was worried for me, and that would be a natural reaction for her. I could hear her voice, and I'm not sure if it was the pain and stitches, or fear, that stopped me from shouting downstairs to my wife to let her in. I heard my wife curtly explain that I was ill in bed and not to be disturbed. But that was my relationship at that time – with both of them. A nursing wife and a caring mistress. I was just about still in love with my wife, but genuinely cared for my swan. It occurred to me then that I was incapable of being genuinely in love with anyone. I was in love with the Job though, I knew that.

After my swan left, my wife told me I'd had a visit from a girl she thought was one of my prostitutes from work. That hurt a bit, but I believe it was designed to.

42

TALKING TURKEY

I did talk to my wife about the Job sometimes. She knew I loved it, particularly my time as a young cop in Vice Squad. I came home just before Christmas one year with a large bag of turkey legs. We were always short of money, and this definitely helped. The legs had been left at the police station for me by a notorious Leeds criminal nicknamed Chopper. He'd served ten years for taking an axe to a previous girlfriend and left her in a terrible state. Why would I take a gift from the type of man I was spending my career trying to put behind bars?

I was having a pint in a Leeds city centre pub that was mainly used by criminals. Of course I was on duty but, as a Vice Squad officer, keeping an eye on pubs and their conformance with the law was one of our duties, even if was a perk too. The landlords of these types of pubs tried to maintain a balance between pandering to the tough guy criminals and not falling foul of us. I liked the challenge of these types of places and wanted them to know who was in charge of Leeds city centre's streets. When I was on duty I was in charge.

I didn't know Chopper at this time, but he elbowed past me as I was waiting to get myself and my vice squad colleague a pint. The landlord looked at us both and served him six pints whilst I looked on, filling with anger. As he took a couple of pints over to his table I took two of his pints back to my table and said 'thanks' to him and the landlord. You could hear a pin drop. His mates all stood up and Chopper told me in a loud, aggressive voice that he'd just dangled his girlfriend by her ankle from the window of their top floor flat for answering him back, but he said his mates had talked him out of dropping her, so they were celebrating. His mates were all laughing at this, but he was angry. A few expletives were involved of course and he told me I was spoiling his celebration — in a menacing sort of way. He told me to bring the pints back to his table. I stood up, picked the two pints up and poured them on the floor. Then I walked past him and ordered two more. The pub was emptying of punters, as they knew trouble was brewing.

It was pure theatre, and I don't know what came over me, but he touched a nerve when he told me what he'd been doing to his girlfriend. I told him to sit down or get arrested. It was incredible; he started laughing and told the landlord the beer was on him. He meant the landlord would pay, because apparently, I discovered later, he never paid for drinks. When I sat down he came over, called me a cheeky bastard in a kind of friendly way and asked me to join him and his mates. I told him I didn't mix with people I didn't like. We drank some of our beer and left the pub and I waved at him as I left. If I'd thought in advance about what I was doing I'm sure I would never have done it, but my automatic reaction to my Achilles Heel had my mouth in action before my brain kicked in. My partner wasn't too pleased either, because he was one of the studious types in our office whose only aim was to use the Vice Squad as a stepping stone to promotion. To him I was a liability.

I saw Chopper around the city pubs over the next few months or so and while we never got close enough to speak, we were on nodding terms. I don't think either of us wanted to push our luck and perhaps end up losing. I was advised by colleagues in CID, who had heard the story through their own contacts, to be wary of him, as he was pimping prostitutes and was known for being a nutter in drink. Probably a bit like my dad, but instead of giving coins from our rent money to children in the street, he preferred giving turkey legs to police in the Vice Squad.

Some months after the spilled pints incident, just before Christmas, I was back at Millgarth Street going off duty when the Station Sergeant called me over and gave me a large, heavy and sealed heavy-duty plastic bag. He didn't know who it was from or who'd dropped it off, but it had my name and 'Vice Squad' written on a tag stuck on it. I went back to my office and used a knife to open it up a bit and nearly fainted. I thought it was full of body parts! Closer examination revealed its true contents. I put the bag in one of the cells, which was as cold a place as you could find, and went home.

Leeds indoor and outdoor market was only a hundred yards from Millgarth Street and after I'd questioned some of the meat stall holders I was in no doubt the legs had come from there. The pub where the beer was spilled was next door to the market. I wasn't a detective at this stage of my career, but I had enough brains and sense to come to the conclusion that Chopper was either trying to frighten me or apologise. I chose the latter in my own mind and decided that as I'd turned down his generous offer of buying two pints, I'd take the turkey thighs home and tell my wife they had been given to me by one of the meat stall holders.

I saw Chopper on many occasions over the next year or two, usually in the rough pubs, particularly the ones used by prostitutes, and he was always pleasant, if not quite deferential. Many of the criminals I associated with during this time told me he thought I was good copper. I was, and I would have loved to have had the opportunity of locking him up. He'd done ten years for chopping his girlfriend up and he thought he could say pleasant things about me? I missed my chance, but I heard years later when I was working in Bradford that he'd gone back home — to prison.

The turkey legs were tasty and welcome. I frequented the meat stalls shortly after that incident and regularly bought pieces of meat for Sunday dinner, always at a discounted price.

43

GUNS AND TOILETS

▪▪▪▪▪▪▪▪▪▪▪▪▪▪▪▪▪▪▪▪▪▪

A good example of my impetuous, or reckless behaviour—
call it what you will— can be well illustrated by what
happened one night during my vice squad time in Leeds city
centre. My partner and I were radioed to attend a posh
multi-storey hotel and speak to the duty manager, who was
alarmed that he had witnessed a man with a gun in the
main bar on the top floor.

Naturally we were in plain clothes. We met the manager
in the top floor bar and had a glass of beer with him as he
told the story. The manager was agitated and complained
that a man had been seen to drop a handgun in the bar
before picking it up, holstering it back under his armpit and
leaving the bar in a hurry.

Suddenly he looked up, horror-struck and said, 'That's
him, he's come back!'

I was six foot tall, slim and fit. He was the same height as me but broader, wearing a cream suit and a fedora hat, and seemed to exude confidence as he approached a couple of women who sat at the bar. We sat staring at him as he looked around the room, until he focused on us – three men, one in a suit and obviously one of the hotel managers, and two others dressed very casually, staring straight at him. He turned quickly and walked towards the exit at the end of the bar away from us. The manager got up and walked away just as quickly. My colleague suggested I stay and watch in case he came back and he would call for the armed response, and off he went behind the manager.

After a couple of minutes I went to the exit door, paused only slightly to take a breath and opened the door. What I didn't know was that the exit door was also the way to the toilets. As I stood in the corridor the toilet door opposite me opened and the man with the gun stood facing me in his cream suit. We were only a couple of feet away from each other and in each other's way. There was immediate eye contact. I carried my warrant card in the outside breast pocket of my jacket and I fished it out and said, 'Police officer. Put your hands in the air.' How corny was that! Other men walked past us as my warrant card came out, and as I pushed it towards him he duly put his hands up. So far, so good. I told him I was arresting him for breach of the peace. This was always a favourite of mine when I was stuck for a power of arrest. I started to put my warrant card back in my breast pocket, and I suppose because I didn't have a plan and I was shaking a bit, I couldn't locate the pocket. I momentarily looked for the pocket and pushed it in. At the same time as I was searching for my pocket, he reached inside his jacket and out of the corner of my eye I saw him pull a revolver out of a shoulder holster.

This, I've come to realise, is where my enthusiastic naivety and determination get mixed up. I leaped at him just as the toilet door opened and we both went flying past a couple of men leaving the toilet. We fell onto the toilet floor, with me holding his gun hand with both of mine and screaming 'Police!' at the top of my voice. He was struggling like mad and we skidded across the floor into the long wall urinal. Men were jumping out of the way, but significantly no one stopped to help or even to watch. We were both trying to head butt each other and he was pulling my rather long hair with his free hand. It was all knees and elbows and foreheads, with me shouting at him that he was under arrest as both of us writhed about in the urine trough.

After a couple of minutes of scrapping, the gun was in the urine trough at the other end of the toilet and we were hitting each other as he tried to escape. Suddenly the door burst open and armed officers arrived with their guns pointing at both of us. I was losing the battle by this time and he was on top of me when I saw the Cavalry over his shoulder.

He was very professionally thrown onto his front, handcuffed and dragged out of the toilet, still with two officers' guns pointing at him. It was over within a couple of seconds. I was hauled up from the floor by one of the officers, almost as unceremoniously, and then confronted by the Armed Response Inspector. He put his face up to mine, holding the recovered revolver even closer, and said, 'You stupid bastard! It's loaded. You could have been killed.' I heard his mate say, 'Should have been if you ask me.' He came and stuck his face into mine and said, 'We deal with gunmen – not you!'

It was no good trying to explain that I hadn't done it on purpose, and besides I was completely out of breath. My trousers and jacket were wet through with urine. I was bruised, battered and scratched and in a state of shock as I walked back into the bar. A lot of guests had left the bar but there were plenty of others looking me up and down like something the dog had dragged in.

My colleague was there with the manager and he told me we had to go back to the police station to see the Night Superintendent. I gave my statement to an inspector and was taken home in a police car, as it was felt generally that I was unfit for further duty. The driver stopped the car on the way back so I could throw up, as what had happened began to dawn on me. Sheila was at that time six or seven months pregnant with Diana. Everything that could have gone wrong with that incident flashed through my mind. I also remember thinking that I should have told the Firearms Inspector and his sidekick to bugger off!

I also made the mistake of not telling my wife about it, although that decision was made in good faith. When the gunman's court case was heard a few months later, just before the birth of our daughter, I was given a court commendation for bravery, and one from the Chief Constable. Mind you, the Chief Constable spent more time lecturing me about the sick leave I'd taken to recover from my gangrenous appendix operation. He said, forcefully and with a hint of anger, that he didn't want to see any more sick leave from me for at least five years. Thank you sir, I remain your obedient servant!

The details of the gun incident were in that evening's *Yorkshire Evening Post*. I got home that tea time to be faced with a war party of wife and in-laws demanding to know what I'd been playing at and why I didn't talk to my wife about things that happen at work! I told them I thought I'd done the right thing by not causing Sheila any distress during the pregnancy. That's what happens when you plan things, it seems to me. I'd thought about the possible consequences of upsetting my heavily pregnant wife with horror stories, made up my mind to remain tight lipped, and I still got it wrong!

The court case was also reported in the *Derbyshire Times* and neighbours were quick to take the paper round to my grandma's house – and she wasn't too pleased with me either. But I loved my life, even though it I can see now that I was selfish. Being in the Job in the sixties, seventies and early eighties, at the height of political incorrectness, was wonderful, and I loved every minute of it.

44

A VERY ODD PREGNANCY, BUT A HEALTHY BABY

Sheila and I were very lucky to have our first child, Diana, born hale and hearty, despite my abysmal efforts to protect Sheila from the stress caused by my exploits at work. A hale and hearty birth wasn't what we were expecting, even though we were desperate for one. Seven or eight months or so earlier, not long after we found out Sheila was pregnant with Diana, we'd been at a neighbour's house celebrating New Year's Eve and dancing when she screamed and fell to the floor. There was blood everywhere and we were taken to hospital by ambulance and eventually told she had miscarried. We were devastated. The next day my friend from across the road asked me to pay for the cost of replacing his carpet. We agreed to share the cost in the end.

When I picked Sheila up the following day the consultant told me that they had had to clean out Sheila's womb using a spoon-shaped instrument to scrape the remains of the foetus out. He said this procedure was often referred to as a scrape. He happily advised us that she could get pregnant again in the future. Giving me what I thought was a rather stern look, the consultant told me that he knew what policemen were like and I was not to have sex for a couple of months until she had got over the trauma of the scrape.

Two months later we were back at the hospital worried that Sheila had not had a period and that her stomach was swelling as if she was still pregnant. It turned out she was. It transpired that she had been pregnant with two babies. She had one womb, but it was split into two, separating the two foetuses. She was either having twins, or I believe he said that she had probably conceived on different occasions and one baby gave up the fight, as it were. We were both alarmed of course that the 'scrape' might have damaged the remaining baby at two months. He said it was possible but unlikely, and that the "divider" had prevented the "spoon" from touching the stronger, more developed baby, seeing as the baby was growing normally. He said the divider would stretch and break as the baby grew and the womb would behave as normal. Thank goodness for experts, but we were constantly worried until she was born, healthily.

These events, scrapes in more ways than one, whilst traumatic to say the least, brought Sheila and me closer together as a couple and we both looked forward to the birth of our first child. I was there at Diana's birth and was delighted to see that her little arms and legs and spine looked normal. Her head didn't though, because it was a difficult birth and forceps had to be used to pull her out. The loose plates of her skull had shifted from round into the shape of a clown's pointed hat because of the pressure of the forceps. The nurses said it was acceptable and that her head would soon look normal. It did regain its normal shape, but it was a fearful time for a while.

I had a special relationship with Diana from the first day and found it easy to bath her, change her nappies, feed her and sing to her. I was very fond of the Stylistics and played the record, 'You Are Beautiful,' and sang it to her constantly.

Something was not right though, and after a year or so Sheila diagnosed herself with postnatal depression. As she was nursing again I had no concern about her knowledge and ability to do a self-diagnosis. She asked me to take a week off work and look after Diana while she went to Clay Cross to stay with my Mam, in order to help her recuperate. I thought it was odd, but I enjoyed my time with my baby girl.

Diana was a happy child and we went out in the pram for hours. She loved bouncing up and down for ages in a bouncy swing fastened to the top of the doorframe into the front room. I was concerned after a couple of days that I had not seen a dirty nappy, though we had regular wet ones. I explained my concerns to Sheila when she rang each evening, but she told me not to worry. She was a nurse of course, so I believed her, despite being a mother for the first time.

On the third or fourth day I picked up an awful smell and quickly recognised what had just happened. I felt a sense of relief. She was happily gurgling away bouncing up and down in her swing on the doorway. Loose stinky poo was squirting out of the top and back of her Babygro, into her hair, down her back and front and onto the carpet every time she bounced. She looked so happy. Now there's a challenge for a new dad.

It turned out that Sheila wasn't suffering from post-natal depression at all. She was missing the sex she had been enjoying with her boyfriend from Harrogate. He was driving down to Clay Cross every evening and taking her out. I had been blind to it, and of course, everyone blamed me for her having an affair, including my Mam. I asked if it might be fifty fifty, but everyone agreed her behaviour was definitely my fault for not being a better husband. Sheila and I persevered though. She promised to dump her boyfriend, a vicar's son can you believe, if I was more loving and spent more quality time with her. I was and I did, for a significant time. Fatherhood definitely changed my attitude quite a bit, for quite a while.

We had our son, Robert, fifteen months after Diana was born. Sheila promised me one hundred per cent that he was mine, and as he grew older he was my double, so there were no doubts. I'd voiced my concerns about parentage to Sheila many times during our first pregnancy, usually during an argument about something irrelevant. I don't think either of us wanted to push it too far because we were both really excited about becoming parents for the first time. Monogamy would have been a good thing in those early years of marriage, but for lineage purposes only. Although I knew growing up in Clay Cross that my future lay elsewhere, I knew my time with Sheila was not destined to last. I thought our relationship, which now included two beautiful children, was working quite well, and, compared with my own father, I thought I was quite a good one. Well, that's probably not a relevant comparison to use, but I knew plenty of other police officers who, in my opinion, didn't appear to be decent fathers.

45

BRADFORD DRUG SQUAD

Moving on a bit, and not for the first time, as you may have noticed. I applied to join the force's Drug Squad based in Bradford, and was accepted. I left Vice Squad in Leeds for a better place! Bradford in the mid-seventies, although our work took us far afield, was a fantastic place to be based, if you craved excitement. My life was a kaleidoscope of events on and off duty and I don't think strict chronology in this book will change anyone's opinion on my disturbing life, or disturb their train of thought, but some of my memories of my time in Drugs Squad just bubble up in no particular order.

Here are but a few. Friendships were forged. Reliance on partners was critical. These were required in a number of life-or-death situations, but just as importantly they were needed when humour, laughter, long hours, tension and sexual relief were de rigueur. I hope as you read my memoirs you are able to conjure up visions that help you share my life and if you think I haven't described in enough detail some incidents, now that you know me you can fill in the gaps yourself.

On one occasion while in Drug Squad I was first officer, responsible for coordinating a complicated case at Wakefield Crown Court involving a massive file of evidence on many defendants. I think there were 24 men accused of various offences involving importation and supplying Class A drugs, firearms and other serious offences. The arrests had been spectacular, with assistance from Customs Officers based in London, who were keen to be involved in the large-scale importation from Pakistan we had uncovered. The network was huge and complicated, but the main criminals involved were Bradford based.

During my cross examination one of the defence barristers asked who had provided me with the information that started the ball rolling. I refused to tell him, and after repeated requests I said I would never give the details of an informant to anyone. The Judge intervened and told me that if he asked me I would have to tell him or be in contempt of court – for which he could send me to prison. I didn't speak, and the court went quiet. The defence barrister asked me again for the informant's details and I repeated that I would not give those details to anyone.

The Judge adjourned the court for half an hour and asked the prosecuting barrister to bring me to his chambers. I was expecting at least a serious telling off and some threats, but he asked me, in a genuine manner, why I was behaving this way. I was gobsmacked that he didn't understand that my informant's life would be at risk if I gave his name out in open court. Not to mention how my own personal credibility would be ruined, in any future relationships with informants. I explained also that giving his name out would in turn reduce future arrests and convictions of seriously evil criminals. This was the way of the world I lived in and I even said something along the lines of keeping people safe in their beds, and that judges and magistrates should let the police get on with their jobs. That was frowned on by the accompanying prosecuting barrister and he held his hand up, indicating I'd said enough.

I suggested in the politest way I could that he should sample the real world or at least listen to stories off the record from seasoned police officers. We had a cup of tea and he gave me the impression that he'd enjoyed talking with me – rather than at me. It wasn't that I didn't respect authority, as many people said, but rather that I seemed to be able to circumvent it without getting into too much trouble. But I thought it would be better if judges were forced to spend some time studying at the university of real life before getting dressed up in their garb and pontificating.

When the court was resumed the Judge immediately told the defence barrister not to ask me that question again. It was as simple as that, and my own reputation was enhanced within the judiciary and those watching from the public gallery. I was even taken out for lunch by the prosecuting counsel at the end of the successful trial – by which I mean that the nasty men went to prison!

In that same trial, during which I spent every day for three consecutive weeks in the witness box giving evidence and being cross-examined, one of the barristers, who had been brought from Jamaica to represent one of the defendants, tried hard to ridicule me in an attempt to lessen the gravity and weight of my evidence. It was a regular ploy when the defence was limited – attack the credibility of the police officer, try and make him angry and appear unreliable. We had our own responses of course. This was my fourth consecutive day of being cross-examined and I was quite relaxed. This man was very theatrical, sweeping his black gown around him with a flourish in front of the bench of jurors whenever he thought he had made a valid point for his client, most of which were about my alleged poor memory. A lot of his questions resulted in my replying that I couldn't remember, or it was something I was not aware of. I was being evasive, waiting for his clever question that must surely arrive. He himself was getting exasperated and suddenly told the jurors that I was a man who obviously took precautions. Before he could come out with his question, I asked the Judge what my sex life had to do with the defence barrister. There was uproar in the gallery and the judge banged his gavel repeatedly before standing up and leaving the Court for his chambers. The defence barristers were seething and the prosecutors laughing – but only after the Judge had left the court room.

When the court resumed, the defence barrister from Jamaica came out from behind his desk and stood directly in front of the witness box where I was, and for at least a minute he just stared at me without moving. I stared back at him. It was all very theatrical and the whole court room waited with bated breath. He eventually said he had a very important question to ask me and I must be prepared for the consequences. He waited for a long time again, staring at me, then started his question, with, 'You are Acting Detective Sergeant Clements?' and once again with, perfect timing on my part, before he could continue, I agreed and said I could remember that. The air was electric anyway and again the whole courtroom exploded with laughter. I didn't move a muscle and continued to stare at him. He was ready to explode, and there was no point in him speaking because no one would have heard him above the cacophony of noise.

When the usher had brought everyone under control the Judge suggested to the barrister that if he didn't have any relevant or pertinent questions to ask of the officer he should sit down and let the case move on. I was already well-known by magistrates and solicitors and barristers, but this took me to a new level and for months I was asked to go through the story again over coffee and beer breaks.

46

MEN IN TIGHTS, AND
THE BEVERLEY SISTERS

Moving ahead again, to one late turn shift in Drug Squad, my mate and I had been asked to take out a young policewoman who was posted to our department for a few weeks. She was working with us under the term 'aide,' to give her experience of serious plain clothes squads. This was to help her when or if she had to deal with something whilst on patrol that might be connected to our role. As we drove through the city I asked her to take her tights off and pass them to me. She refused at first, but I explained that they were needed immediately and eventually she handed them over to me in the front passenger seat. My penknife cut through the crotch and I handed one leg to my mate, who put it over his head. I did the same and we stopped at half a dozen bus stops in the city centre and asked people in the queue if they could direct us to Barclays Bank. I know, it's childish, but it was a prelude to some serious police work, knocking doors down and arresting violent drug abusers and pushers. But those moments were priceless, and even the policewoman laughed eventually. To my knowledge, no policeman had ever been convicted of impersonating a criminal!

I don't want anyone to think I was a sexual predator, although as I'm writing this I'm beginning to wonder, but another brief interlude involving this young lady in my life is worth mentioning. My Drug Squad partner and I were eating in the police station canteen in Bradford and chatting to a uniformed inspector friend of mine. We were sitting next to a very attractive policewoman who seemed to be hanging onto our every word as we discussed some recent drugs raids.

On the spur of the moment I told my friendly inspector that we were currently carrying out some serious drugs surveillance in Keighley and could do with utilising an unknown policewoman to help our disguise in some of the pubs in that area. He immediately suggested, with an imperceptible wink, that we 'borrow' his new young policewoman for a few weeks and that it would be good experience for her and perhaps create some enthusiasm in the rest of his team to follow in her footsteps. What a great idea. My partner and I agreed immediately and asked if we could start that evening, but advised her that she wouldn't be eligible for overtime. She was as enthusiastic as we were and off we went, following her home so she could get changed out of uniform and then on to Keighley for a drink or two and some surveillance.

After a week of working together we discovered we had a lot in common. She had an excellent memory for faces and a dark sense of humour; she was fit, had no fear, loved take-away Chinese food and loved sex. One thing led to another and we started an affair. Every time I dropped her off after working with us, a couple of times a week, we had different take-away food but the same sex.

One night after our usual bout of bedroom gymnastics, about a month after we'd started working together, she told me in all seriousness that her sister, a teacher, who had split from her husband months earlier was desperate for sex. She said she'd told her sister about us, and how enjoyable it was and that I was discreet. Then she knocked me out by asking me if I thought my partner, a married man though soon to be divorced, might come back to her house after work with us and shag her sister!

I'm not easily shocked, but I was for a short time, until I visualised the potential situation – a lounge and kitchen on the ground floor, a bedroom (hers) on the first floor and an attic room directly above that. There was nothing clandestine or awkward in her suggestion, or rather her proposal. When I pointed out the living accommodation, pointing to the ceiling above us, she laughed and said she was her sister and she was desperate.

It took all of half a sentence to convince my partner. He didn't believe it would happen but was game for a laugh. We did our usual surveillance, but with an extra pair of eyes. The schoolteacher joined us in the pub and made it a two-couple surveillance, which was much better from a practical work aspect and perhaps something we should have thought about before. My lover made the introductions and we watched, drank, talked and watched some more until instinct took over and we all went to the small mid-terraced three up, three down mad house, taking Chinese food with us as sustenance.

My police sister took the initiative and led me by the hand out of the room and to her bedroom. We were followed a few minutes later as the schoolteacher sister obviously did the same and led my mate past our door to the bedroom in the attic directly above the one we were in.

My partner and I were used to taking risks and competing with each other, but this was great. They were about eight feet above us in a direct line and their bedsprings, and other noises, were often noisily in unison, until theirs suddenly raced away from us and after a few joyous shouts and grunts, it went quiet, apart from our bedsprings and other noises carrying on. Of course it did culminate in a crescendo, followed by a loud voice from my partner, feet above us, accusing me of having to win at everything, followed by lots of laughter.

This was followed by more of the same for quite a few months, before and after work, but always with a lot of laughter and energy. But all good things come to an end, they say.

It stopped when my partner and I arrived in the Drug Squad office one evening to start work. As we walked through the office door, the day shift coppers were all lined up against the far wall and started singing the Beverley Sisters' most well-known song, 'Sisters, sisters, never were there such devoted sisters...' This was followed by uproarious laughter from them and jeers from the CID office next door. My partner and I valued our jobs and lives and we made that night, or the early hours of it, our final foursome, but not without a few tears and plenty of regrets from both bedrooms.

47

DUSTBIN LID SHIELDS

▗▖▗▖▗▖▗▖▗▖▗▖▗▖▗▖▗▖▗▖▗▖

It seemed our drug squad team, but particularly me, and whoever my partners were at any time, lived life on the edge constantly. An informant gave me reliable information about a big drugs deal going on in a house in Bradford, and within the hour we had a warrant. The informant said at least two of the suppliers, from Liverpool, were armed with revolvers. Our squad of six got together at the back of the Victorian terraced houses armed with a sledgehammer and handcuffs. Stab vests and suchlike hadn't been invented then, or certainly not issued to police officers. Anyway, who needs a stab vest when you've got adrenaline coursing through you?

We needed all six of us to enter the house at the same time to create the fear effect unexpected raids cause, so we decided we would all go through the back door. Of course we would have had a couple at the front if we'd had the manpower, but we didn't like to share our activities with non-Drug Squad departments. We decided no one inside would have time to respond quickly enough to get to the front door and get away. We were all well-versed in these actions, but as we stealthily approached the house, I picked up a dustbin lid from one of the outhouses. The rest followed suit as we progressed.

We smashed the door in and ran in screaming and shouting 'drug squad!' and plenty of obscenities, as usual, but with our chests hidden behind dustbin lids. The adrenaline rush is fantastic in these circumstances and the look of fear on their faces as they were faced by a small army of dustbin lids was something to remember. No shots were fired and we didn't find any guns, but we did recover a lot of serious drugs and made some serious arrests. There were no car keys either, so they'd obviously been dropped off and the drivers kept their distance.

A learned colleague pointed out to us later how useless the bin lids would be at stopping a bullet, and proved it by piercing one of our trophy bin lids by pushing an HB pencil straight through it. We all said we had been using them to create fear and alarm, not as life savers, but we were ridiculed by many nonetheless, despite the success of the raid.

One of my very reliable informants told me of a big class A drugs supplier and gave her address on the outskirts of Bradford. Amazingly, he told me she was the mother of a footballer playing in the first team of a First Division club (later to become the Premiership as we know it today). At this time I was an avid supporter of Leeds United, and the team this lad played for was a significant rival, so there was added spice.

Unfortunately, my informant also advised me that she always slept with a loaded handgun under her pillow. He even knew which bedroom. Some of my informants were more reckless than I was, and at times like this I often had a fear that I would have to arrest them as well during subsequent follow-ups. The footballer's mother and serious drugs dealer lived in a really big and beautifully-decorated house with large gardens. Even the magistrate granting the warrant questioned the accuracy of my information, simply because of the location. But my informant had always been right and I trusted him. And of course he was well paid. He regularly provided me with recipes for the curries I had when I visited him at his home, and I never suffered food poisoning. Mind you, his written translation of his wife's recipes left a bit to be desired and caused great merriment when I started cooking myself and showed my guests the recipes! My visits to him were always clandestine of course.

We had our usual six Drug Squad team and we all felt slightly nervous as we climbed over other residents' hedges and walls to get to the suspect's house. Not because of the possibility of a gun being used, but because the house didn't fit the usual profile of a serial drug supplier. There were no dogs, no bars at the windows, no flash cars in the drive and no security lights. It was so grand and the lawns and flower beds were so well manicured. In fact, her house looked same as all the others in the area, or better. There was some jealousy on our part too.

I convinced everyone we were good to go and that the suspect would be on her own. We all knew which room we were going to race into once the door was knocked down. Because the information had come from my informant and I was the officer in charge, I allocated the suspect's bedroom to myself and the detective policewoman I was partnering.

It might have been a posh house, but the front door caved in just like all the others and my colleague and I ran straight upstairs and into her bedroom, with everyone doing the usual screaming and shouting. It even occurred to me that I should have wiped my feet on the entrance door mat. Our timing was spot on and our suspect was only just beginning to sit up when we burst into her nicely-decorated bedroom.

My colleague, Lorraine, an Amazonian beauty with an attitude, coupled with the addition of her own fear, adrenaline and excitement, dragged the suspect out of her bed very unceremoniously within seconds of the door crashing down. I went for the pillow next to where she had been sleeping. My informant was right. I gingerly pulled out a Smith & Wesson revolver from under the pillow. And it was fully loaded. We also recovered a significant amount of drugs, but she said very little, in her house or on the way to the Bridewell.

We left her in the cells for what was left of the morning and we all went home for a few hours' sleep. My Amazonian colleague and I interviewed her together for hours, without a solicitor. She said she didn't want one and would be pleading guilty to everything. She was a real character, intelligent, full of humour, anecdotes and great to interview. One of her most memorable comments was that she would look my partner and me up after she got out of prison — and take us out for a meal! She admitted everything to do with the supplying of the Class A and B drugs we recovered, but insisted the gun was not to shoot policemen with – only other drug suppliers who might take her for an easy target because she was female. She said she'd only fired it once, just to make sure it worked.

She told us she supplied mainly in Liverpool and Manchester rather than her home town of Bradford, and because she didn't trust the villains over the Pennines she needed a gun to feel safe. She always carried it under her car seat when driving and in her handbag when she was dealing. She didn't want to create any attention for herself, but in particular she didn't want to draw any adverse attention to her son, who she said she loved and admired, but that he was better off living with his dad. She kept her word, quietly pleaded guilty to everything and spent the next five years in prison. We all admired her. And of course my informant was significantly financially better off as a result.

We were always busy making arrests and carrying out raids based on our own observations and enquiries as well as responding to information from informants. No two days would be the same, unless you were office-bound preparing the files. Although we had our own typists from the pool dedicated just to us, we also typed up hundreds of our own statements and those of witnesses to speed things up. But one telephone call from an informant, or a secret meeting in a pub, could change everything. An urgent meeting of the team, decisions made and warrants obtained within the hour and off we'd go again, leaving mountains of paperwork behind to be caught up with again as soon as we could. We had a great saying in our squad when we weren't sure if we had quite enough evidence or information, or if opinion was slightly divided, which wasn't very often. It wasn't about tossing a coin, or saying shall we, shan't we, and it became folklore – 'faint heart never fucked a pig.' And with that off we all went, racing to the scene with sledgehammers, cuffs and attitudes.

These sorties were a welcome break from preparing court files, when you might spend twelve hours a day for a couple of weeks preparing the files. One memorable case involved thirty-five defendants for serious drug supplying and the files of evidence had to be transported to court in so many boxes they filled a Transit van.

48

THE REAL-LIFE PUNCHBAG WHO COULDN'T BE KNOCKED OVER

▀▞▀▞▀▞▀▞▀▞▀▞▀▞▀▞▀▞▀▞▀

There was always a potential for danger when arresting someone who didn't want to lose his or her freedom. My partner, my regular male one, and I knew of a drugs deal going down in the heart of the red light area of Bradford late one night. We'd been on duty since early afternoon and should really have gone home, but locking this bloke up was worth any amount of effort. We'd been after him for years and never had a proper sniff. The rundown and in parts derelict area was always busy with prostitutes, pimps, druggies, drug suppliers, drunks and cars being driven slowly around, always containing one male, looking for an expensive sexual thrill, at any time of day or night. But night time was always more thrilling.

It was well after midnight. The pubs were closed but the cafés and shebeens were fully loaded. We saw the suspect, again believed to be from Liverpool, stop his car and hand over a package to our own suspected drug supplier. I raced the squad car up to them and the car sped off. Our man ran, but that's a loose description, as he was as wide as he was high. But it was dark where they'd done the deal. He made it round a few corners, then back onto the main road. We easily caught him and his left hand was clenched tightly. We grabbed a fist each, as he started shouting loudly in a kind of ululating voice. He was so strong he threw my mate over a nearby wall as if he was a child. My mate won't want to read this, because he was fit and a good footballer, even though he did smoke and drink too much, but the suspect was too strong for him.

I had a decision to make and quickly, before he could use both his fists on me, and because my mate was still lying on the other side of the wall, dazed. We'd shouted we were Drug Squad as we jumped out of the car, but in any case he knew me, and I knew he would not come with us quietly. By now a lot of local people were approaching us from the cafés, shebeens and nearby houses and most of them were what I would describe as undesirables. I suppose their mothers would disagree with my description, but if there was a vote involving the judicature we would win hands down. Anyway, I looked at him, weighed up my options in a split second and hit the suspect as hard as I could with my fist, aiming for his face, and caught him a ringing blow in his eye.

He was about five foot six round, with a head the size of a football and, begging his mother's forgiveness, pug ugly. I saw his eyes roll into the top of his head, but he just stood there rocking backwards and forwards. My mate clambered back over the wall and joined me and together we pushed and pulled him to the drug squad car and shoved him onto the back seat. He was coming to and tried to escape, leaping upwards and forwards to get out of the car door, trapping my hand between his head and the top of the car door frame. I could feel my fingers breaking and as I screamed I jumped on him and we fell back into the car. My mate drove off with our feet hanging out of the back seat.

What I hadn't noticed was how many people were about to grab us. As we drove through the crowd men were leaping onto the bonnet, pulling the window wipers off, trying to open the driver's door and pulling at my legs and our prisoner's legs. It was a nightmare in slow motion. Fifty yards down the road we had left the crowd behind, some of them lying or sitting on the ground, and I could hear the sirens and see the blue lights flashing as colleagues belatedly arrived. The crowd of angry men and women quickly dispersed.

After the prisoner and I had been treated by the police doctor, who then joined us in the canteen and shared a hip flask of his special concoction in our coffee, my partner and I both agreed that we could have planned that job better. We made a pact that in future we would try not to put our lives in danger.

A few months later, during the Crown Court trial of the man who couldn't be knocked down, while driving to work I saw that all the full-size billboards outside newsagents, and on the street corners where vendors were selling the *Bradford Gazette*, carried a copy of the front page emblazoned with the words 'Detective punches man in eye – alleged'. The best thing was that the weeble didn't bear any grudges and even laughed when he was telling everyone that because the skin around his swollen eye was so stretched and pale, he was a black man with a white eye.

Planning was always difficult for me. Mostly I seemed to get better results through spur of the moment decisions. Not always of course, and one particular incident of recklessness almost resulted in police and public being hacked by a large angry man with a machete.

Lorraine, the policewoman who'd been my bedroom partner in the arrest of the footballer's mother and was fairly new to Drug Squad at the time, was strikingly good looking in an Amazonian way and she became my partner for a while. I was first to be her working partner because I'd been in the squad for a few years and she needed to be trained and become trusted. I was still only in my late twenties, my wife and I staying together for the sake of our children, as they say — and I was no doubt a loose cannon in many colleagues' eyes. This woman was six years younger than me and mainly because of her looks and personality, had led a charmed life, in and out of the Job.

From the first day we met and started working together, my one and only ambition was to make love with her. It became an obsession with me because she constantly turned my approaches down, but was nevertheless good company, and she was determined to become a good Drug Squad officer, which I admired. I became infatuated with her, particularly as other members of our squad were letting it be known over the months that she had slept with them. I wasn't put off. As you will have realised by now, I can be rather foolishly stubborn and determined, regardless of potential personal consequences.

I was out with her one night and we were hiding behind a wall at the back of a well-known West Indian café, the Blue Moon, in the centre of the red light area in Bradford with a view into the café through the kitchen window. We were keeping observations on known drug suppliers and their associates using the café. I was pestering her to kiss me and she was resisting. We were there for the best part of an hour, which gave me time to persist a lot. I was feeling frustrated and even a bit put out, and then suddenly we clearly saw the owner of the café put her hands up in the air as if she was being threatened. We also clearly saw a large man waving an enormous machete around in an arc. Everyone gave him space but he was directing his anger towards the owner, Blossom. I knew her well and she was a lovely woman, just wanting to earn enough to look after her big family. She and her brother had even brought me a bottle of extremely toxic rum back from Jamaica earlier in the year, as a 'thank you' for some trainers I'd given her eldest son.

I paused for a second, taking it all in. Then I turned to my very attractive Amazonian partner, looked at her red lipsticked lips and told her if she didn't kiss me straight away I was going to go into the café and rescue Blossom. She said 'No!' three or four times, with her voice rising all the time. Before I had time to think about what my mate and I had discussed only weeks earlier about planning, I was up and over the wall, running down the alley and bursting in through the front door shouting my usual, 'Drug Squad!' at the top of my voice.

The café was packed, especially near the front door, but there was a decent gap near the counter where Blossom was standing. I pushed my way through, continuing to shout. I saw Blossom crying and the back door open and immediately began to pray that my non-kissing partner had not decided to block his escape. I was pleased to note she was right behind me, having taken the longer route to the front door, as she admitted later that she couldn't climb the wall like my athletic self. The machete wielder was gone. All's well that ends well, as they say, and we were treated by Blossom to bowls of delicious West Indian chicken and rice, which was somewhere between supper and breakfast time. Blossom gave me a good imitation of a Mrs Meredith hug, and called me an idiot.

What could there possibly be that's not to love about this job? The 1970s was a great decade for me. And it got even better when my Amazonian partner finally got round to ticking me off her list. The passenger seats in our Drug Squad cars saw some action over the next few months, and I knew all barriers were down when she agreed to a sexual fantasy of my own. During one of many blow jobs she gave me, I asked her if she would take out her four top false teeth, attached to a plate, to see if the blow job might be more sensational. She agreed eventually and handed me her dentures, insisting that I held them as she tried it out. Once again I reminded myself about thinking things through before committing myself to action, and after staring at the teeth on plastic, quickly asked her to put them back in!

My relationship with my sexually appealing and approving partner had reached the point where I believed being married to her had potentially far more benefits than my current sexless married relationship, despite having two beautiful young children aged three and four.

49

SHEILA'S DEPARTURE

Sheila walked out on me one day, out of the blue, to go and live with her son-of-a-vicar-from-Harrogate boyfriend. And that was despite my visit to him one night, months earlier, threatening to break his legs if he ever saw my wife again. When I got home from visiting him at his house in Harrogate, thinking that would be the end of any future relationships, she greeted me with tears and tantrums and threats - for frightening him! He'd had the gall to telephone her and complain about what had happened.

She left the children with me, and I took time off from Drug Squad with the blessing and support of the Detective Inspector. He was a fan of mine, but I owed him one because he called it 'special leave.' Sheila phoned me every night to talk to the kids. They didn't understand what had happened and kept asking for her. I repeatedly asked her to come home, but she blithely told me she was enjoying herself and her new-found freedom to go out for drinks and meals in Harrogate with her boyfriend. He obviously didn't value his legs. Her mum and dad came round to give advice and some help, but I didn't need them.

After a couple of weeks Sheila returned home with her parents. I wouldn't let her in and kept the door locked. I systematically threw her clothes and personal belongings she'd left behind out of the front bedroom window onto the lawn. The neighbours were all out watching and listening to the shouting match. I refused to let her in despite the local police inspector attending and threatening to have me sacked. I gave in after a few days, and with support from her mum we agreed to make another go of our marriage.

We put the house up for sale and agreed we would buy a smaller one and use some of the profit for a second honeymoon to Kenya. We moved house three months later to a smaller one in Otley and set off to East Africa on a cold February morning. It was my first ever trip abroad, and we were both massively excited. My Mam looked after Diana and Robert for us and she was hopeful that a 'second honeymoon' would be the answer to our marriage problems. I thought it would be too, and had great expectations.

It was fantastic. We went to big game reserves and snake pits, swam in the Indian Ocean and I even went deep sea fishing and caught a massive tuna on a rod and line, strapped into a big comfy chair at the back of the speed boat with no land in sight. The lovemaking was a bit disappointing for a honeymoon, but I discovered the reason for that when I examined the bill on our last day. The most expensive charges for the whole fortnight were the daily telephone calls to the boyfriend in Harrogate.

It was a quiet flight home and despite her promises that

she would give him up, our marriage ended. She took Diana and Robert to live in Clay Cross near my family, because her own weren't too keen on her behaviour. With a bit of free help from a friendly solicitor's firm I knew through work, we agreed that I would pay her out and keep the small terraced house. The honeymoon period with the vicar's son didn't last long either. He gave her up quickly because he didn't want children, and certainly not ours.

Perhaps I should explain about my second marriage here before this kaleidoscopic portrayal of my life gets too complicated to follow. My soon-to-be second wife might have been a bit tall with plenty of curves, in all the right places, and some plastic teeth, but her lusty, gung-ho attitude to life really appealed to me. It had the potential to be a match made in heaven, if you look on the bright side of life, and I always believed my glass was half full.

A friend of mine from my Leeds City Police days was also my dentist in Bradford. He'd replaced my own single false tooth, which was fitted to a piece plastic housed in the palate of my mouth, with a permanent bridge some years earlier. What a difference that made to my life! All police officers will tell you that spending hours in a witness box being cross-examined by well-educated barristers who would rather see you in prison than their clients can be a bit daunting. Especially when your mouth gets dry. When this happened, my denture lost its adhesive, my tooth became loose and would start to 'clack' and move up and down as I spoke. Saliva was a rare commodity under these circumstances, as were coherent sentences, so after his dentistry my confidence soared and sentences flowed, even during the most harrowing hours in the witness box.

I'd sold up in Otley and bought a house near Bradford,

closer to work, and I'd explained to my dentist friend about my future wife's missing top four (without advising him what she was capable of doing when they were removed) and asked him if he could help. He convinced me that he could do for her what he'd done for me, at a price. We agreed that I would have her use him as her dentist and introduced her to him. He was a charmer with a top of the range Porsche, so she took to him straight away. We agreed that he would convince her she was getting four better-looking false teeth, again attached to a plate in her palate. He did convince her of this but during all the visits he was secretly measuring her up to be fitted with a permanent bridge.

It did occur to me that I might be cutting my nose off to spite my face here, but the thought of taking them out again one day for possible pleasure, compared to them not moving around a bit during passionate kissing, swayed it. It cost a fortune, but when he did the surprise final fitting and she came home to me ecstatic and smiling like a Cheshire cat, it was worth every penny. She said her gain was at least four times better than mine must have been.

We should have lived happily ever after, but the usual infidelity struck us both, although we did wait until we married. Well, I did.

50

DEMOTION - A BLESSING
IN DISGUISE

▀▗▀▗▀▗▀▗▀▗▀▗▀▗▀▗▀▗▀▗▀▗▀▗▀▗

While I was on holiday with my newly-bridged and smiling future second wife, I was demoted. What a shock I had when I went back to work. Well, I wasn't actually demoted whilst away. I engineered that quite easily myself after I refused to apologise, or even admit I'd done something wrong. I'd been set up whilst working on one of the many Yorkshire Ripper enquiries. As you have probably gathered by now I lived for the Job, and although I sailed quite close to the wind at times, I would never jeopardise anything on such a serious enquiry as the Ripper investigation. I suppose in a way I deserved to incur the wrath of the man who set me up. He was a fellow officer with a very pronounced stutter and his name was Danny Kaye. I foolishly laughed out loud when a colleague said, in front of many people, 'Speech therapy rules – O K-K-K-K-Kaye!' It was genuinely funny, and as an ex-stutterer I can understand him being upset, but I don't think it was worth setting me up for. I'd tried to help him years before when I told him I'd had a stutter and told him what I'd done to make it better. He told me to 'F-F-F*** off!'

I had asked a colleague on the Ripper enquiry to take a witness statement I'd prepared in advance to the witness and get it signed. I'd taken the witness's words over the phone to prepare the statement. The investigation was going nowhere. The witness had seen a car parked in his cul-de-sac one night a few weeks before one of the Ripper's attacks and didn't know who it belonged to, but loose ends had to be tidied up, and I was going on holiday the next day. My colleague then gave it to someone else and he to someone else, and before long it ended up in Kaye's hands as a statement for filing, signed by me but not signed by the witness. He made a banquet out of it, saying I was cheating and lazy and no wonder we couldn't catch the Ripper when I couldn't even get a statement signed. I was furious, loudly, and made a scene in an attempt to clear my name, and I refused to back down.

I was given the opportunity of apologising to him, and I refused of course. It was escalated to one of the inspectors, and then to a chief inspector. I flatly refused to apologise and be condemned. Everything was out of proportion, particularly when I was told to go to headquarters and see the Assistant Chief Constable, George Oldfield, and apologise to him.

Oldfield's secretary let me into his massive oak-panelled office. He sat slouched, head on his forearms over his large desk. No saluting as we were obviously in plain clothes, a very smart suit for me and a crumpled one for him. I, and many others who regularly worked on the Ripper enquiries, had no time for him. He was a two-bottles-of-whisky-a-day man and when he decided to put all our eggs in his one basket, claiming the Ripper was a Geordie on the strength of what turned out to be a hoax call, we all groaned. He was just not up to the job. Committed, yes. Believable, no.

Anyway, he had the temerity to make his opening statement something along the lines of, 'It's because of people like you that we can't catch the Ripper'. I wonder where he'd read that. It was like pouring petrol onto my already inflamed sense of injustice. I'd lost a wife and two children recently due to my love of the Job and no one worked longer hours than I did, more often than not for free, so to hear those hurtful words was more than I could stand. He told me to get out of his office and get a uniform because I was no good as a detective. I lost control and leaned over his desk, shouting at him that he was the wrong man for this enquiry, that he was a drunk and a joke. I said a few more words and plenty of adjectives, but as sentences they wouldn't have made sense. I'd lost it.

I stormed out of his office and slammed his door. His secretary had heard it all and was standing up behind her desk with a look of horror on her face. But I hadn't finished. I turned back to his door and kicked it open and shouted at him that he could stick his job, leaving the door wide open as I stormed out. I sat in my car shaking, and for the first time since my grandma had died a year earlier, I cried, this time out of frustration.

I drove slowly from Police Headquarters at Wakefield to Bradford and went rather solemnly to see my own Detective Chief Inspector to tell him I'd been sacked. He even smiled. He told me he'd heard from George's secretary what had happened and said I should have been sacked, but I was instead to start in uniform at Horsforth Police Station, ten miles from where I was living with my soon to be second wife, the next day. And to go and get a uniform.

What a comedown! I actually reported for duty at Horsforth Police Station the next day, and saw the Sub-Divisional Officer (SDO), who, luckily for me, had been a Detective Chief Inspector at Millgarth Street in my Vice Squad days. He was a supporter of mine and told me not to worry. He told me he needed someone on the streets with some experience to train his young officers how to do the job properly, and that he had no doubt he would have me promoted within a year. That was a better start than I was expecting. Although I started my uniform stint the following day on night shift, the SDO took time out to ask me to return to the station whenever he was visiting, for a chat and an update on how I was doing and to talk about the good old days at Millgarth Street. I'd fallen on my feet again.

Incredibly, although I had little interest in cricket in those days, I was sent to do uniform crowd control at Headingly cricket ground the following Monday, 20th July 1981, as Ian Botham almost single-handedly walloped the Aussies to help win the Ashes. I became a cricket fan that day and have loved it ever since. I was in fact the officer seen on the perimeter of the pitch throwing his helmet up in the air when the final ball was bowled. Talk about one door closes and another one opens!

Apparently the bridges I'd burned were rather big ones, and I was the subject of conversation on many police officers' lips in my first couple of months. I was sent to work in the Kirkstall area of Horsforth's sub-divisional area as a Community Constable. The SDO asked me to go there as the crime rate was out of control and he would give me free rein to sort it out. Within a couple of weeks I had photos of myself printed with historical and current information about me stuck on telegraph poles, bus stops and schools so I would be known quickly by the local population, the good ones and the bad ones. It worked, and I was soon invited to all the local schools, community centres and associations, even Gingerbread meetings for single parents. I spoke about my aspirations to improve the community and the well-being of all who resided in my area. I asked everyone to approach me with any of their trials and tribulations, and insisted that no one should ever ignore me.

I quickly identified the ringleaders of the kids responsible for vandalism and anti-social behaviour and soon had them under my thumb. It was a quick way of getting support from the community and I had at least a hundred 'tea spots' within a few months. I attended functions and events, spoke freely and shook a lot of hands, but more importantly I banged a few heads.

I don't want to dwell too much on this time of my life, because although it was extremely rewarding, for me personally and apparently for many residents, it wasn't exciting enough to keep anyone reading my memoirs to keep turning the pages over. However, those who know or knew me personally at that time would disagree and would suggest this was one of the most important times of my life.

51

SINGLE FATHER

What I discovered working as a Community Constable, as I calmed down, was that I couldn't cope without my children. I couldn't stop myself driving to Clay Cross from my home in Bradford during a day off, or from Horsforth police station whenever my shift finished at 2 pm, arriving just in time to see Diana and Robert walking out of their school at 3.30 to meet their mum and walk home. They never saw me parked up nearby with binoculars and it drove me crazy every time I saw them. I could tell how unhappy they were and I knew from comments made occasionally by my own family, who all lived nearby, that Sheila was having a succession of boyfriends visiting and staying at her house and my kids were upset and unhappy. She was also drinking a lot and her behaviour was erratic. I accepted I was in part responsible for their state of mind - it was just the percentage of responsibility I couldn't agree on with anyone. I wanted security and continuity for them, and selfishly decided I could do a better job of bringing them up than their mother could.

I went to see a solicitor friend of mine from my Drug Squad days and told him I wanted custody. He introduced me to another member of his firm who specialised in divorce law. This solicitor told me what to do and said I should represent myself in court to keep the costs down. As a result, after almost a year of being without my children - although I had fixed visits and time with them – and after numerous appearances at Chesterfield County Court, I was granted custody of both of them. Representing myself, I could speak freely about my feelings and reasons for having custody and Sheila, much to her disgust and anger, had her comments and accusations curtailed as she had to let her solicitor speak on her behalf. I'd been given good and free advice and taken full advantage. Even my family, on this occasion, agreed with my actions.

Looking back, if it hadn't been for my fellow stutterer and the Assistant Chief Constable (Crime) I would have remained in CID and certainly not have had the opportunity or time to win back and then look after my children. Again, lucky, or what?

So I inherited my own children. I brought Diana and Robert up myself from the ages of four and five until they were in their teens and left home. My wife at that time, second one, did not help much; in fact she was more of a hindrance and couldn't bring herself to be pleasant to them. But I'd made my bed and there were some good times of course. I was never the perfect father and made many mistakes, but I look back now and wonder how many men are perfect fathers, particularly when they are not sharing their off-springs' upbringing with their real mother.

There were three or four regular families on the estate where we lived who looked after my kids after school, until I collected them when I'd finished work. I often called at two or three of these families, one after the other, apologising as I searched for the ones who were caring for them that particular evening. Not the best method for good parenting, but they were all very helpful and understanding in those days. However I was convinced they were better off with me and after only a couple of months of winning custody Sheila dropped all contact with them. She only saw them again a few times after that until she died a couple of years ago.

My second wife didn't want children of her own, let alone young children of mine, and made it quite obvious to them and me that she was not suited to being a mother. Not a good basis for a successful marriage, and there were a lot of arguments about, and in front of, the children. But I had custody of Diana and Robert before we married, so there was a get-out clause if she'd wanted to take it.

It was in my early days as a Community Constable that I married my Amazonian, at a Register Office in York, followed by a blessing in an old church in York and a reception in a posh hotel there. It was a party! A few members of our families attended but there were plenty of current and past police colleagues who knew our background and enjoyed our party too. And of course my children Diana and Robert were part of the celebration

My best man, John, and I had been best friends since I joined Leeds City Police. I'd been his best man a few years earlier and he'd been a guest at my first wedding. My first best man and his second wife were also in attendance, as he was for my third marriage many years later. I'd also been his best man at his first wedding and a guest at his second.

That's some continuity and support. Complicated or convoluted? Some friends are friends for life.

It was a happy wedding and I got on well with my new in-laws. During my groom's speech I told my mother–in-law she was welcome to visit us at any time, and that I'd even bought her her own personal transport. At that the Master of Ceremonies, as planned, appeared from behind her with an old-fashioned broomstick and handed it to her. She laughed and took it in good part – but kept the broomstick! Eventually my best man did his bit and he was very good, even though he was nervous. It all went well until the infamous toast to the bride and groom. Dear John, you are forgiven. Come and meet my new one – she's called Karen. Practise the name if you are going to visit!

52

BMXS AND SMALL URINALS

So, on with my time in Kirkstall as a Community Constable. An old house had been knocked down in the middle of Kirkstall and it was an eyesore. A surgery and chemist's shop were to be built on it at some stage, but it was the meeting place for the youthful petty criminals. It was the size of a school playground, but it had been left for months, and kids played on it and sometimes threw stones from it at cars passing nearby. I asked them what they needed that would help them enjoy the area rather than create local havoc. Most of them had BMX bikes and wanted a race track.

This is where coming from a mining community comes in handy. I asked some builders nearby to bring one of their small bulldozers over and shape the uneven land into hills and valleys. I set off in the police station's public order van, with a like-minded colleague who'd been there and done it all, to a colliery near Doncaster. I was trespassing really, because Doncaster was in South Yorkshire Police's area and I should have sought permission from them to enter their area. Whatever — it was for charity. I'd telephoned and spoken to one of the pit managers and told him what I was after. He just said 'you can have it if you collect it'.

My colleague (amazingly after all this time, the one who'd called me 'love' and I'd apparently call 'duck') and I pulled up in the colliery yard and amidst many ribald comments from miners dressed for work down the pit, loaded up what I needed. Many of the miners also helped and when I explained what I intended doing they were very gracious with their comments. My colleague and I returned with the van laden with rolls of heavy-duty rubber conveyor belts. Kids came from all over Kirkstall to help unload and lay it out over about two hundred yards of sculptured mounds and hollows that ended up resembling a circular track, three feet wide. The kids were riding their bikes fast and furiously, uphill and down dale, round corners and hairpins before it was fully laid.

It was a quick fix and a fantastic result, and I was a hero with the kids and a lot of parents. So much so that the next day my SDO told me to go Kirkstall Middle School to see a reporter from the *Yorkshire Evening Post*. That evening my face was on the front page of the paper with a lad on a BMX sailing high over my head. Clever photography, but it looked fantastic. And the article was well written, but I got a bollocking from my friendly SDO for not telling him what I'd been up to. I'd raised the profile of Kirkstall as a place to enjoy living and also the profile of our police station – without a senior police officer in sight!

The headmaster of Kirkstall Middle School thought

what I'd done was brilliant and asked me if he could introduce me to his pupils at assembly, when I could give them a talk on good behaviour. See how things have changed — me lecturing others on how to behave!

I went the next morning, shiny boots and best uniform, but I stopped at the school toilets after being directed there by a pupil. I then made my way to the large assembly hall, again after asking directions from a pupil, thereby entering the hall from the wrong end. All the pupils were watching me expectantly as I walked past them approaching the stage from the wrong direction, where I was met by the headmaster and his teachers. I apologised for the delay and said I'd used the kids' toilets on the way in. The headmaster quickly remarked that I would always be considered as staff and could always use the staff toilets in future. It was an ice breaker, but I said I preferred using the small urinals as they made my willy look bigger! Some of the staff laughed out loud and others looked at me as if I should be arrested. Of course the children didn't know what was going on as they looked up at a rather disorientated group of teachers.

I took the opportunity to tell all the children that I would be watching them and that it was their duty to be attentive school children, pass their exams and behave themselves after school. I also told the children they must never hide from me, and when they saw me they were to be polite and call me Mr Clements and to tell their parents to do the same. Everything was just so easy and rewarding and I was appreciated every day by lively but respectful kids and lovely, pleasant adults. There were some exceptions of course, but I soon found them alternative accommodation!

My reputation for getting things done spread like wildfire. One day I attended a house where two elderly widows lived, in an area occupied predominantly by rowdy kids and drunken adults who had no respect for this elderly pair. They'd lived there most of their lives and seen it deteriorate and were ready to give up and stay indoors all day and night. I went to the local housing officer, asked to see the person in charge and convinced her that these two should be moved to a new estate nearby where I was sure they would live together in one house, thereby freeing up two others where she could house some more low life. She said my approach was unorthodox, mainly because I said I would support them in front of a newspaper reporter I'd got friendly with, so I was committed to doing so.

I helped them with their removal and into their new house, and it took two weeks. That small deed brought them so much happiness, and it was a joy to pop in for a cup of tea when I trespassed over the road to the other divisional area where they lived. When I got promoted and left the area a couple of years later they came to my leaving do and presented me with a briefcase, because they thought a police sergeant would need it! I've still got it and think of them often.

I was invited to speak at the other local schools over the next couple of weeks as a result of schools sharing information, but the request was always with a proviso to use the staff toilets and visit the head's office before going to the main hall. I was greeted by children and parents with, 'Hello Mr Clements.' at least a hundred times a day. My life in those days was MAD every day – Making A Difference.

53

DOG'S DINNER

▜▚▜▚▜▚▜▚▜▚▜▚▜▚▜▚▜▚▜▚▜

My normal everyday life was not matched at home by my Welsh Springer Spaniel, Ben. He really did have a death wish. He just couldn't help himself from getting into trouble. No matter how many doors I closed before going to work he managed to open them. On returning from work I would call his name and get no response. His favourite place in the house was my bed and when I eventually went upstairs he would be lying on his back baring his chattering teeth, his lips quivering like a nervous smile and his body shaking. Knowing he'd been caught in the act, he was too frightened to move, despite my verbal threats, and I always had to pick him up and carry him downstairs. He continued to pretend fear until my verbals and finger wagging had finished and then he'd find and carry his lead to me and off we'd go.

His appetite for walking and racing around the local

arable fields disturbing birds and rabbits was only matched by his appetite for food. His food exploits were legendary in our community. I once made a big pan of super-spicy curry the day before some friends were visiting, but as is my wont, forgot it was on the burner. The pan was beyond repair and I took it outside and left it near the dustbin. I intended to bag it up when it had cooled, but forgot.

A short time later there was a frantic knocking on our back door by a friend who shared our drive. She and her two children were laughing hysterically and pointing at Ben, who had climbed up their outdoor water barrel, hanging onto the top with his front paws, scrabbling to stay on with his rear ones and lapping the water furiously. Then, as we all watched, he jumped down, ran over to the pan of curry, licked at that just as furiously for about ten seconds, then raced back across the drive to the water barrel, scrabbled up it and drank more water. We all stood, either speechless or laughing out loud, attracting other neighbours who came over to see what the fuss was all about. When he lay on his back, baring his teeth and shivering like a guilty dog we realised all the curry had gone, apart from some tomato skins left in the bottom. What entertainment!

Many of the neighbours then told me they fed Ben with titbits every day when he called to see them on his rounds, and my next-door neighbour told me she set a place for him at their table and he sat with her and the kids at some meal times! That habit caused huge embarrassment and some anger a few months later. I was at the front of our house one Sunday lunch time talking to the neighbour whose wife fed Ben at their table when Ben strolled down their drive, walked past us with his tail wagging and up our drive. We stopped talking and watched with eyes wide open, because there was a whole cooked chicken in his mouth. His mouth and lips were so stretched to hold the chicken, which made him look as if he was grinning widely, like a cartoon character. We were still standing watching disbelievingly, when my mate's wife ran out of her house shouting, 'The chicken's gone, the chicken's gone!'

My wife ran out of our house and disturbed Ben tucking into their Sunday roast, and he ran onto the front lawn. I know it was a stupid thing to do, but I felt I had to do something, so I tried to pull the chicken out of Ben's mouth and he started running round in circles on the lawn. Looking back it is funny now, but he ran round and around with the chicken bouncing up and down hiding his face until I fell over. Every time he was far enough away from me, or I was prostrate on the lawn, he gulped some chicken down his throat and then set off running again. The fear in his eyes only matched the anger in mine, but he wouldn't let go of the chicken at any cost.

In my own moment of embarrassment, I foolishly started shouting at Ben that I was going to take him to the vet's and have him put down. This made my wife cry and my neighbours were insistent that it was okay, they would have sandwiches for lunch. He obviously realised how serious his theft was, because eventually he ran up the street and out of sight. I went off in my car searching for him and told my wife and neighbours that when I found him he was going straight to the vet.

After half an hour and no sight of him I calmed down enough to think I should buy some food for my neighbours' lunch, so I set off to the shops just outside our estate. There was a road block at the exit and although there were a few cars affected it was quiet enough for me to see that my wife had blocked the exit side of the road with her car. I left my car in the queue and walked down to the small group of people consoling my wife, who I could hear telling them she was stopping me from killing our dog!

It all calmed down. I bought some cooked ham and some cakes for my neighbours' lunch and invited them round for a meal the following weekend. Ben didn't come back until late that night. We found him on our drive at the back door lying on his back doing his usual body shaking, showing his teeth and quivering lips. And of course I was made out to be the bad guy in all this. Many years later he passed away in my arms after a lethal injection at the local vet's. I miss him dearly.

54

PANCAKES AND A LEGACY

In my first few months as a Community Constable, and particularly in the school holidays, I was regularly sent to a problem family who were causing havoc in and around the sheltered housing near to their house. The mother of the eight children, ranging from two to sixteen years old, had died in childbirth giving birth to the last, not long after the couple had arrived from Mauritius. The father worked every hour he could, leaving a social worker to call round and tend his kids. The father just could not cope, so staying at work was keeping him sane. I called round many times and befriended the younger ones, who more often than not were all on the floor watching videos. I had to wait until it was raining to make sure I captured all of the family in the house at the same time. And this I had to do plenty of times, rather than walk the streets looking to tackle the miscreants. I did get them under control, and I made them attend school and gave the allocated social worker as much advice and support as I could. She was a neighbour, recruited and paid to look after the kids on a part-time basis. Her wage was made up by the missing father, who was a very honest, gentle and law-abiding man, but no match for his kids.

I called at their house one Pancake Day and they were all, as usual, watching videos or fighting with each other. By now I was accustomed to just walking in unannounced and if I needed to speak sternly about anything I told them to turn the TV off and they did so without a second thought. I always stood in the doorway to the lounge to prevent the older ones walking out, but they were respectful enough for me to get my messages across. On this occasion I asked if they were having pancakes and drew blank looks. I checked the pantry and fridge and there was only bread, cereal and biscuits.

I told them about Pancake Day and took some of the younger ones to the local shop with me to buy eggs, butter, flour, fresh oranges and some sweets for those accompanying me. I'd always made pancakes at home, so I knew what I was doing. It had been a tradition with my grandma, who made her mixture in the washing up bowl and made as many as I could eat. I just had to be careful with the amount of sugar and oranges because money was always tight, but as soon as I was married I bought loads of oranges and my pancake days were always memorable.

I found the largest pan the family had and used a three-pound bag of flour and all twelve eggs. There were only three plates and a couple of knives, forks and spoons in the house, so I lined them up from oldest to youngest like a dark-skinned Von Trapp family. As soon as they finished, they handed their plate to whomever was next in line and went to the back of the queue. The smell and atmosphere were brilliant. My ingredients soon ran out, so I sent the two eldest to the shop for more supplies – and sent them back again an hour later. I was there all afternoon and it was one of the most rewarding, pleasurable and funny things I've ever done. I'm sure I could have stayed all night and they would have carried on collecting, eating and going to the back of the queue. I really hope they do the same for their kids now they're grown up.

It's amazing how little things like this caught on with adult neighbours. Many not only appreciated me controlling the kids, but some referred to me, courageously I think, with the nickname 'Mr Pancake' for a while. It was great fun.

When I told the family I was leaving the area to go to Bradford on promotion, they were all genuinely upset. One of the community groups bought me an inscribed pewter tankard. I still have it, amongst many other leaving gifts. The local art shop owner presented me with a limited edition painting I'd always admired when I visited the shop for coffee. It's always had pride of place at the top of the stairs in the five houses I've lived in since. On the back in his own bold and neat handwriting he'd inscribed: 'It just goes to show – you can fool all of the people all of the time!'

I met and treasured some wonderful people during this period of my life and it was all very rewarding. However it was not exciting enough for a young, fit bloke in his late twenties with an attitude. Looking back I ought to have stayed there, with my captive and respectful audience, two young children at home, a very obedient Springer Spaniel and a very hot (or very cold) wife. But I closed the door on that episode and opened another, and did it without a sideways glance, let alone a backward one.

I had my leaving/promotion do at the local Conservative Club, on my patch, where the Committee had insisted on making me an honorary member, mainly because of my ability at snooker I think. Both floors were packed and there were large groups outside, not able to get in but still managing to get served beer and drinks. It was a very emotional leaving do and the *Yorkshire Post* even sent a reporter, so my face was in their paper again the next day. I found out the next day that the Chief Inspector whose shift I would be joining in Bradford shortly had heard stories about me and invited himself to my leaving do to run the rule over me. He couldn't get in, nor could my SDO, who was supposed to be saying a few farewell words on my behalf. Instead, speeches were made by teachers and staff from local schools and community groups. The SDO did return when people started leaving and had a couple of pints. He thanked me for what I'd done for his area, and he was genuine too.

I had a great time there and not one affair – well, not a sexual one but a love affair. I reduced the crime rate, re-routed the futures of many kids, helped a great community pull its socks up and take pride in itself and took a treasure chest of pleasant memories with me.

A few months after I left to become a uniform sergeant at Bradford, I was invited back to the opening ceremony of the purpose-built BMX racetrack the council and local communities had jointly paid to be built in the woods behind Kirkstall church. Fantastic! What a legacy.

55

PROMOTION AND TATTOOS

Any promotion in the police means leading by appearance ie. stripes on your arms or pips on your shoulders, or by commitment ie. knowledge, experience and by example. I almost came unstuck on my first night shift. I was getting to know my team and during the parades before the shift started, or at meal breaks and I would be questioned enthusiastically by some of the team who were the get-up-and-go types. I told some of them that I saw in them a mirror image of myself at their age. This encouraged them to go out and get the job done, but it made them ask even more questions about my history.

I was asked on this particular parade by some of the youngsters what to look for in order to do a successful stop and search. I told them, rather flippantly, to watch for ugly men with tattoos, jeans and trainers who were smoking. I told them they would invariably find drugs or a weapon of some sort. Not long after, the pubs were turning out one busy Friday or Saturday night. I was called over the radio to quickly go and see a constable who was having difficulty with a crowd in the doorway to Boots the Chemist in the city centre. I asked why and was told the officer wouldn't say what was wrong but had requested me personally and to hurry.

I used a blue light for the first time (I hadn't spent much of my police service in marked cars) and within a couple of minutes I was nosing through a large throng of revellers in the pedestrian precinct, all facing Boots the Chemist. I had to push my way through forcefully to get to the front and saw my worst nightmare – an officer just managing to hold a man in the corner of the doorway. His mates were pressing to get him released and there was a lot of shouting and swearing. I had enough presence to calm things down a bit with the crowd and told the man to calm down and stop swearing. I had the situation virtually under control. The bloke started shouting and struggling again and said the officer had no right to search him. With a sinking feeling I asked the officer why he'd stopped him to search him, and he said confidently, with a smile on his face, 'because he's ugly and he's covered in tattoos'!

The volume from him and his mates went up considerably and a few fists were flung, while many of the drunken onlookers gave their opinions about his ugliness. None of it helped the situation. My saving grace was recognising the bloke he'd stopped. I'd arrested him for drugs years earlier and he'd even been a part-time informant. When I asked him quietly into his ear if he remembered me, he said he did. I reminded him of the nickname I had been falsely given and he remembered that too. I told him to give the officer his name and address and that would be it, he could go on his way. I said I wouldn't search him if he agreed to this. I'm sure he would have been carrying at least some cannabis and my offer to not search him carried a lot more weight. He agreed, gave his details and calmed his mates down and off they went. The officer kept his credibility, although he was bouncing with the excitement of it all. I took him with me in the Panda car until meal break so I could talk to him, explain things a bit better, and calm him down.

My young, impressionable policeman and many others on the shift regularly asked me how I had calmed the man down and got him to give his details. I never told them, because I'd now learned a valuable lesson about making glib comments. I didn't tell them either that my old nickname, given to me by some of the people I'd arrested in Drug Squad, was The Gardener, implying I was good at planting things. I never discouraged criminals from thinking the worst of me, because reputations, good or bad, can help in many ways. If I'm face-to-face with a criminal, I'd rather him fear me than the other way round.

56

SHEBEENS, SCARS AND RUGBY HEROES

Not long after this incident, I was missing the excitement of working in plain clothes or under cover and I suspect I was behaving a bit recklessly, even for me. I was celebrating a win at Leeds Crown Court resulting from a couple of arrests I couldn't help making, even though as a uniform sergeant I was supposed to be leading and teaching, not actually doing. To celebrate my sense of achievement I foolishly took a couple of police colleagues from Bradford out for a drink that evening. I was still in my Crown Court suit, the one I'd worn for my second wedding; baby blue gabardine material and very smart, but worn on this occasion to exude extra gravitas to impress the jurors and Judge in Court. I was high on the adrenaline of success, the defendants now languishing at Her Majesty's Pleasure, and I had had too many drinks.

It was this state of mind that encouraged me to show off to my subordinates and take them to a shebeen in the red light area to finish the night before we went for a curry. They were excited about visiting an unlawful late night drinking establishment and I was happy to be their leader in this little adventure. I was generally proud to lead them on normal working days as their sergeant. I was a fool to lead with the wrong attitude on this occasion, but as usual, heart first, brains later.

The shebeen was mostly full of law-abiding and decent male West Indians, with plenty of prostitutes and a few drug dealers and users I recognised. I felt an unwelcome atmosphere immediately, which sobered me up considerably, but not quite enough to stop me looking around to see the cause of it. I should have led my young men back out of the door and gone for a curry.

I left my colleagues near the bar and went upstairs. This was a mistake, because suddenly one of men I recognised as having arrested back in my Drug Squad days shouted repeatedly, in a very loud voice, 'Clements just called me a black cunt, Clements just called me a black cunt!' I hadn't spoken to him or anyone else. It was obviously orchestrated and a gang of them rushed at me. I dived under the pool table as they threw pool balls at me and tried to hit me with pool cues. They used the cues to prod me out and I fought with them to get to the top of the staircase in a forlorn attempt to escape back downstairs. There were sixty or seventy men in the upstairs room and about twenty of them were determined to tear me apart. They all wanted a bit of me and we were a tightly-knit throng. That obviously helped me as it was difficult for anyone to land a telling blow, or so I thought.

Looking back now, thirty odd years later, I think of what happened to PC Keith Blakelock and realise just how much my life was in the balance. My attackers were obviously using this moment to get revenge for time spent in prison because of my past actions, but they were definitely creating this diversion to allow the drug dealers and their drugs to escape.

Through the melee I could see one of my colleagues climbing up the wide staircase to help me. He wasn't in fact climbing the stairs, which were thronged with men and prostitutes also trying to see the spectacle; he was actually climbing on top of their shoulders and heads, on his hands and knees. We fought and punched at anyone grabbing us and we fought and scrambled towards each other, as the music stopped and the lights came on. It was total confusion.

For every man I hit with punches, the other officer was hitting at least two, but when he hit someone, they stayed down. He was a constable on my team, but more importantly he was the current Bradford and England Rugby League Captain and the fittest and most muscular man I'd ever seen in a gym.

He eventually reached my hand and pulled me towards him as the owners of the club and some decent regulars started to clear the staircase and pulled us down to the entrance. We were rather unceremoniously pushed outside and the door locked and bolted behind us. We sat on the pavement and saw our other colleague standing near the wall. He'd been pushed out earlier, thank goodness. His eyes were large, his face was very white and he had difficulty speaking. I was out of order to take someone that young and inexperienced into a shebeen. But I'm pleased to say that he went on in later life to become an inspector, running teams of his own, and talked about this incident as one of the highlights of his career.

There is no doubt in my mind that my muscular rugby captain saved my life. I was normally very effective using my tongue to deal with potential and actual serious issues, but it helps if you are sober and your brain is in gear. That night these faculties were missing and I endangered many other peoples' lives, not just my own. Thanks, Brian, you were a true and courageous friend when I needed one.

It was further confirmed that my fairy godfather rugby league player had saved my life when I stood up from the pavement, brushed myself down and tried to fasten my jacket. It felt loose, and my mates cried out when they saw I'd been slashed with a Stanley knife down my back. The cut was from my collar to my belt, and I was lucky that the blade had apparently not been fully extended. The cut was all the way down the side of my spine and bleeding. My brain eventually kicked in and I took control, hailing a passing a taxi to take us all home, dropping me off last as I offered to pay for causing their trouble. They agreed with my request not to talk about what had happened to anyone. The last thing I wanted was to be the cause of the shebeen being raided and more officers and innocents being hurt. So I lived with it.

The scar remained for years, particularly when I sunbathed, and the line that ran the full length of my back slice stayed white, or lighter than the rest of my back. I was in even more trouble with my wife when she found out what I'd done, and she was even angrier at me for throwing my wedding suit jacket in the dustbin. I told her I was keeping the trousers for golf, but that didn't stop the verbal onslaught. I think most wives, under these circumstances, would be relieved their husband was still alive. But you learn from your mistakes. Oops! Did I just write that? Of course I didn't mean it— I have *never* learned from my mistakes.

People talked about me being a brave or courageous policeman, not because my idiotic behaviour got me knifed but generally. But I wasn't. I just reacted to circumstances, or situations I created or involved myself in, without thinking things through, But, against the odds, I invariably got away with it.

I do believe there's a medical description for what I suffered from. It's called automatism. I learned at training school in my first months as a constable about a solicitor who famously represented a well-heeled client who'd crashed his car and was charged with driving without due care and attention. The solicitor said his defence was that he'd had a sneezing fit and lost control of his car. He explained that the crash was a result of automatism – an automatic response to a sensory nerve. Some say it is 'acting from the spinal cord.' I rest my case!

I like to think that the short time I spent as a uniform sergeant, working with a load of young and impressionable police officers, was informative and worthwhile for them. Many of them stayed in touch with me, seeking my advice by telephone and personally - and not just about police work but their home lives as well. I'm not sure I helped them with those problems, but at least I made them better police officers.

We had a seasoned uniform policewoman working at our station who was, to say the least, well-endowed – in fact 'voluptuous' would be a better description. Her bust would appear through the doorway seconds before the rest of her did. She knew it and revelled in it. She could hold her own with any seasoned policeman, or criminal or drunken lout. On night shift she often asked for any new male recruit to be put with her so she could walk her part of the city and show him the ropes. At meal times the recruit would always come in starry eyed and be in love with her, invariably because she'd shagged him in a shop doorway in some dark alley. I suppose it could be called initiation. She never entertained any of us older ones though, despite the begging. Don't forget this was still the eighties and political correctness hadn't been born yet.

57

VICE, WITH RESPONSIBILITY

■▼▲▼▲▼▲▼▲▼▲▼▲▼▲▼▲▼▲■

I didn't have to spend too long in uniform before I applied for, and was given, the responsibility for managing Bradford's Vice Squad. It was a step up from what I did in Leeds Vice Squad because I was in charge, but I knew I would have to temper my wild side and use my experience to lead by example. I was now in my mid-thirties and well into my second marriage, and around this time probably well on my way to leaving the marriage too. I dealt with hundreds of prostitutes and their pimps on a daily basis, in the same area where I had had some of my memorable scrapes when working as a detective in Drug Squad. The more prostitutes I and my team arrested, the more I realised that they were the victims of crimes, not the perpetrators.

I was genuinely sympathetic to the girls' situations and a lot of them knew and respected me for this. Many of them came to trust me. Some of the better-looking ones said they were often asked to help the punters live their sexual fantasies rather than the usual blow jobs and intercourse. One girl was the 'go to' girl if the punter wanted a girl to urinate over him as he lay on the floor masturbating. Others wanted the girls to wear high heels after the punter had urinated in them. These punters were normally well-heeled themselves and not only paid for the service but brought the girls decent shoes and left them with them. Plenty just wanted a good spanking, or to be led around the car park by a ribbon tied round their penis. Some of the girls said they were being well paid for getting their own back on men in general!

One memorable prostitute was in fact a bloke, a young man who dressed as a young woman. He made a lot of money and, as well as becoming an informant for me, helped me to groom some of our younger officers in the art of never taking things for granted. When we took on a new recruit I would take that officer, male or female, into the red light district and by arrangement arrest the male prostitute masquerading as a woman. He would do the usual, in front of our spying eyes, waving a shapely leg from of a mini dress, or bending down and blowing kisses to passing motorist, until we had seen enough to prove she was a common prostitute soliciting for the purpose of prostitution under the Street Offences Act 1959.

By prior arrangement with the station sergeant, we would take the prostitute to an interview room until he was ready to book 'her' in. I would ask the new recruit to sit with her and talk to her about her behaviour and try to get her back on the straight and narrow. Then I would lock the door to the room and leave them to it. Within five minutes we could hear banging and shouting from the interview room as the recruit listened to the prostitute telling the story of how he made his money. He would go into graphic detail about needing money, dressing as a woman, and telling the clients when they had reached their destination in some remote care park that 'she' had started her period, apologising and asked the punter if he would mind shagging her up her arse. He would tell the young officer he always got a good tip for this and made plenty of money and loved his job because he didn't have a pimp and kept all of his earnings. And of course the recruit, knowing the law, would quickly point out that we had arrested him for being a common prostitute – and that only applied to women!

I would unlock the door and ask what all the noise was about and the recruit would be babbling about the prostitute being a man and saying we couldn't arrest him and he was a pervert. So we let him out of the back door with advice about his future behaviour – until the next time he was needed.

Just in case you're wondering, the answer is no, I never did, although I was propositioned constantly by the girls and they all wanted to be the first. I had a soft spot for them all. I even suggested to a bench of magistrates from the witness box one day that instead of perpetually fining the girls for prostitution, they should suspend the fine and if they did not re-offend within three months, the fines could be quashed. They liked my idea, because they realised the girls were only having to work harder, or more often, to pay the fines and still provide their pimps with the cash they'd become accustomed to.

One of the senior magistrates approached my Chief Superintendent shortly after my suggestion asking if he could arrange for me to give a presentation to all the Bradford area magistrates on prostitution and my ideas to improve the situation. I glibly agreed, only to be told later that over a hundred of them wanted to attend. I was advised that they would open the court concourse and fill it with chairs. It was the talk of the station and I was even approached by some magistrates, during my regular court appearances, to be told they were looking forward to my presentation. No such thing then as Powerpoint and lap tops. And hopefully no such thing as a stutter!

The best thing was, I wasn't worried about my stutter, just the content. And it couldn't be a ten-minute talk. I was told to make the presentation last for one hour and plan for another hour of questioning. The Chief Superintendent declined to attend, telling me I'd only got myself to blame, but wished me good luck. I had an idea though. It would need two large televisions, one on each corner of the stage, on tables so everyone could see, running simultaneously, playing VHS tapes and I would do a voice-over commentary.

I borrowed a video camera from the Scenes of Crime Department – they were as large as a small suitcase in those days. I had a colleague drive me in a plain car and did a worm's eye recording of the prostitutes working the streets, following the cars they'd been picked up in to the usual spare land where the sex and payment took place. Many of the prostitutes worked outside the houses of law-abiding home-owners and outside the local churches. I made it quite obvious in the video just how many prostitutes were working at any one time of day and evening, and that local residents, churchgoers and children were repeatedly subjected to their behaviour. I also recorded punters stopping their cars and asking law-abiding women on their way to and from the local shops, churches and mosque and school girls on their way home if they were 'looking for business'.

Our office had received many complaints from ladies going to and from work or shopping complaining they were regularly accosted by men driving slowly past them. The magistrates needed to understand what the background was when they had reticent and sorry-looking prostitutes in the dock in their courtroom. I also knew I was going to lose some of my popularity with a number of local solicitors who derived plenty of income from representing prostitutes using the legal aid system.

After I'd shown the Chief Superintendent the video I intended playing, and my idea to talk over the scenes the magistrates would see on the TV screens, he said that having done a worm's eye view, I should utilise the force's helicopter and do a bird's eye view to put the geographical vice area into perspective. What a great idea! I asked him if he would be going up in the helicopter, and he just wished me luck.

He gave permission and I went to Wakefield, twenty miles and a one-hour drive from Bradford, in the Vice Squad car, carrying the borrowed video camera. I returned to Bradford in a small helicopter within a couple of minutes, containing the pilot and a very eager and enthusiastic 'scenes of crime' officer, with his own latest state-of-the-art video camera. A hundred miles an hour from Wakefield to Bradford was bad enough, but when I showed them the vice area he hovered over it, tilting it this way and that to get a good view as I waited for it to fall out of the sky. The SOCO fastened a spare belt to his own trouser belt, tied it through the seat and leaned out horizontal to the ground, asking me to hold him around the waist to make sure he was safe as I was buckled into the seat. I was beside myself. I've always been scared of heights. Being in the 'copter with the doors shut wasn't too bad, but now! He had his legs dangling out and was shouting instructions to the pilot to fly at 45 degrees and "crab" so he could get better shots. It was supposed to be just aerial shots of the prostitutes' area of operation, but when we examined his work of art in his office later, there were plenty of upturned faces staring at us, many of whom I recognised as my prostitutes! He was good at his job though, and edited my worm's eye view offering and his own into continuous scenes. He then duplicated the finished video a couple of times, so I could show two simultaneously at either end of the presentation stage at my presentation and give the spare to the missing Chief Superintendent.

I have to say, as modestly as I can, that the presentation went exceptionally well and I received a standing ovation afterwards. But I was passionate about my job and the role I was playing, so it wasn't that difficult. My absent boss told me the following day that he'd had a meeting with the senior magistrate, who had given him a glowing report on my presentation and said it was a shame he couldn't make it! It was said with plenty of tongue in cheek. The best thing was, the magistrates took on my recommendations. They also showed a lot of interest in the cases and took time out to talk to the prostitutes with some compassion and knowledge of their difficulties.

The pimps, as well as being very violent, were also business savvy. We were pleased at the very noticeable reduction of working girls in the red light area until we discovered that the pimps were transporting them to Leeds and Wakefield and sometimes Sheffield and Hull, until their fine suspension was up and they could work in Bradford again. Still, it was a move in the right direction and it did get me on Yorkshire Television when they were doing a big piece on prostitution, along with one of the vicars, who was extolling my virtues to anyone in authority and to newspapers who would listen and take an interest. He saw me as a concerned Vice Squad officer helping to look after his flock, not as a good husband. I saw a lot of this vicar during my stint in Vice Squad, attending and supporting his views at the many meetings he arranged, and I even told him I'd invite him to my next wedding.

I spent many hours not just dealing with prostitutes and crawlers but getting to know them and to try and find out their backgrounds. I genuinely wanted to help many of them. Seeing some girls as young as thirteen working the streets for pimps made my blood boil. I was always picking them up and taking them back to the children's homes they'd escaped from and spending time with them, their social workers and sometimes their parents. When they did eventually believe in me and tell me about their family background, it sickened me to discover that almost all of them had suffered sexual abuse by their fathers, brothers, uncles and other relatives. I did save some, but nowhere near enough to be proud of my achievements. In many respects, my time in Vice Squad was a sad time, but very memorable and of course exciting.

58

BASTARD PIMPS

I worked hard and spent a lot of time trying to improve the lives of some of the girls who I thought might be turned from the life they had been forced into — not chosen, as many police and public think. I was very keen to get the pimps locked up and sent to prison where they belonged rather than deal with the results of their greedy and malicious disregard for the girls' lives. I eventually encouraged one of the girls to trust me and open up to me about her life story and what happened behind the scenes with their pimps. I promised her that if she would give me a written statement about her pimp, and talk another couple of girls into doing the same, I would find them nice houses outside Bradford. I promised I would give them a new life and provide them with support and at the same time send their pimps to prison.

Four of them came to see me and said they would do it. They were all in their very early twenties. I had already discussed their situation, and my feelings and opinions, with Social Services, the Probation Service and Housing Departments and knew I could keep my promises to change their lives and keep them safe, so what happened next still makes me feel sick and furious in equal measures.

I didn't have commitment or significant support from my superiors when I told them the lengths I was going to to give the girls a new life. They were keen on me arresting and sending the pimps to prison, but they thought I was on a wild goose chase trying to change the lifestyles of the prostitutes. Saying that perhaps I should have been a nurse rather than a police officer was my tongue-in-cheek reply to anyone who didn't agree with my proposals to help these girls escape from the hell on earth they lived in.

I dedicated over a month to taking the girls into my confidence, giving them self-belief and confidence and then writing out their statements. Listening to their stories was sickening. I thought I was hard enough to deal with most things and related my feelings at this point to my beautiful swan's bullying situation, but I discovered this violence was at another level. Depravity doesn't do it justice. Watching the girls cry and hold each other as they related their stories was heartbreaking. They had never dared tell these stories to anyone until they sat with me. They were too ashamed to discuss their horror stories and situations with what family they had left that they could till speak to, or even to any friends they had left. They couldn't even share the horror they suffered with their colleagues, because they were fatalistic enough to know it could get even worse if their pimps found out. It wasn't even cathartic for them. It just reopened their wounds and on a number of occasions, over the weeks they were with me, they said they couldn't go on.

These young girls feared for their very lives, and I could see why. Sometimes they left my office and didn't come back for a couple of days, but gradually I had the full picture written down, with their signatures on the statements and I was raring to go. I don't believe there is a law-abiding man or woman in the country who wouldn't have taken a gun to the pimps controlling these wretched girls after listening and watching them pour out their hearts and souls.

One of the girls told me that a year earlier, on her 18th birthday, she had asked her pimp if she could have the night off 'work' and perhaps they could go for a drink together. He reacted by punching her in the face repeatedly and screaming at her that he'd spent his 21st in prison, and she was in his prison and belonged to him. She said he tortured her then for the rest of the evening. He made her put her hand on the work top and smashed a hammer onto it. When he told her to put her other hand there, she pulled it away as he brought the hammer down, so he hit her in her breasts with it. He continued to beat her and then dragged her screaming to the bedroom. He tied her naked to the single bed, stood astride her, pissed all over her, then pulled the top of the bedside lamp apart and stood at the side of her and electrocuted her by touching various sensitive parts of her body. All the time he was telling her she was a slut and she belonged to him.

I knew this pimp from my Drug Squad days and had seen him spending money in pubs and clubs like a millionaire. I had goose bumps and shivers as she told me this horror story and I've got them again now, just as vividly, as I recall that horrible time over thirty years ago.

The way she described it and the way she cried when she was telling me had me walking around the office snarling and banging my fist on the furniture. I couldn't wait to get the bastard – especially when she told me he had made her work the night after she had come out of hospital. He'd told her to just do blow jobs until she had the plaster cast taken off her arm.

The other girls had similar violent, harrowing stories, but the vision I had of how he electrocuted her and pissed on her body will stick in my mind forever. Each statement took days to obtain. There were so many stories, and I wanted them to start from their first days as a prostitute. We eventually had some good fun when they trusted me to be able to help them. I would bring meals into the interview rooms and have all four of them together in the room to support each other and share their stories, always with a policewoman present.

It is quite amazing how, in the face of adversity, some people, in line with the jobs they do, laugh, tell jokes and deal with the most serious things in life so light-heartedly. These women were good to work with and talk to, and I know I gave them some fun, happiness and peace of mind for a while and a little hope for their future. But they were also realistic and quite fatalistic. The longer we spent together and trusted each other, the more they confided in me. They all told me that their problems started through being abused by fathers and or relatives as youngsters. It was their lack of self-esteem that was criminal. What a waste of young lives.

Having read so far about the background of these girls, I'm sure you would agree it makes you angry and frustrated. If you are going to read on, I'll warn you now that you will find it harrowing and painful. So before you do, let me explain how I used a sly method to get the girls to relax and confide in me. They did tell me later that this really helped them, although to ordinary people who've lived sheltered lives, you might find my behaviour a bit unnerving.

Sitting and talking and questioning the girls every day hour after hour could be tedious if the results were not forthcoming. I devised a simple plan to help them relax. You can do this safely at home. Take a coat hanger and cut a length of it to about nine inches. Use pliers to bend each end into a U-shaped curve. Then bend the hanger into a bow shape, as in bow and arrow. Take two elastic bands and thread them through a half inch metal washer, then and fasten the ends of the bands to the ends of the coat hanger so it looks like a drawn bow, with the washer suspended in the middle. The trick now, whilst talking to the girls, is to put your hands under the desk and wind the washer round until the elastic bands become taut. If you let go of the washer at this stage you will damage your fingertips, as the washer will revolve at a fantastic speed.

Calmly, holding the taut washer tightly, place the contraption under your bottom and carefully remove your hand. You are now sitting on a tightly-wound washer which is desperate to uncoil itself. With a bit of practice you can slightly lift one side of your bottom, whilst explaining and apologising for suffering from stomach pains because of last night's curry, and allow the washer to rotate at a massive speed, creating friction between your trousers and the vinyl seat and imitating a magnificent fart. With a bit of practice you can do one long one, until the elastic bands have wound down, or lift and shift periodically and let rip short staccato bursts. The effects are incredible.

At first they accepted my apologies demurely, but as the hours passed by and I was adept enough to surreptitiously remove, rewind and replace, their forgiveness was replaced by suggestions on how to prevent wind with herbal remedies and to drink plenty of milk after a curry. Those in turn were eventually replaced by raucous laughter and ribald comments about opening windows to let the smell out. It served to relax them and take their mind off their harrowing stories.

I eventually discovered that just two pimps controlled the four of them as well as, apparently, many other girls who had not come forward. Looking back I think I behaved a bit like a madman for a month or so while I searched for them. They knew I was onto them shortly after their sources of income stopped. I'd found council houses for the girls I considered to be in my care. I made it known to everyone in the red light area and pubs that I was after their pimps, that I had evidence against them and of course they did what cowards do, they went to ground and hid from me. They were animals, and now they were behaving like frightened, hunted animals. I would receive information from informants or other girls regularly as to where one or both of them were hiding. I would go straight to these addresses regardless of my workload or time of day or night. I never knocked and if the door was locked I kicked it in. I had always seen the curtains twitch on arrival so I knew someone was in and suspected it was the pimp I was after, although they were never there when I entered. Until one day.

The houses or flats never contained either pimps or prostitutes, until one day I struck lucky – literally. As I burst in he tried to run past me and lashed out. I defended myself and he received a bruised face. I'd told my colleague to wait at the bottom of the stairs in case he tried to escape. He did, and my colleague picked him up at the bottom of the staircase. He looked a bit of a mess when we arrived at the police station. He made an allegation that I had assaulted him, but later withdrew it.

I had the pleasure of watching him cry during one of the interviews. I read the statements of the prostitutes he'd nearly killed and defiled, and whose earnings he had been living off. Not just living off, but living the life of a millionaire, albeit in the red light area. He wouldn't have been welcome in any other area, despite his wealth and posh car. I read the statements I had taken from them word for word with controlled passion and anger, and hopefully a perceived threat. He wasn't crying because of remorse. He was crying because of the time he knew he was going to spend in prison. He worked out in the gym and could easily have earned a living working on a building site. But he was pathetic – another evil, woman-beating man in my life whom I detested, and I let him know it.

I virtually lived at my Vice Squad office for the next week or so, interviewing and compiling the file for the prosecution. I greatly enjoyed opposing his bail in the magistrate's court and read some extracts out from the girls' statements to show how evil and dangerous he was. Of course there was the usual application for bail from the solicitors, claiming that there had been a witch hunt by me and that nothing had yet been proved. The local papers were full of it. The other pimp came in voluntarily with his solicitor, thereby preventing the arrest I had planned for him.

Both were remanded in custody until their trial at Crown Court. My girls were living well out of the area and two of them had jobs. None of their prostitute colleagues knew where they lived, so try as they might, the pimps' criminal colleagues couldn't force information from anyone and I had high hopes of long prison sentences for the pimps and new futures and freedom for the girls. I agreed that the girls would come to the police station in Bradford on the first day of the trial and I would take them personally to Leeds Crown Court. The trial date was eventually set, but it had taken nine months from the arrest. The pimps had been incarcerated the whole of this time. A small step in the right direction, but a wonderful one.

And then, on the most important day of what would be the rest of their lives, the girls didn't turn up. I was beside myself. I had officers in the relevant outlying areas visit their homes. No sign of them. Neighbours told the officers that they had left the previous day. My immediate concern was for their safety, hoping that their new homes hadn't been discovered by the pimps' criminal associates. I couldn't wait any longer and left Bradford to go to the Crown Court in Leeds and speak to the prosecuting barrister. I was both furious and concerned about their disappearance and discussed my fears and frustration with the prosecuting barrister. He told me the two pimps would walk if I didn't bring the witnesses.

Our prosecuting barrister spoke to the Judge in his chambers before the trial was due to start. I was called into the witness box by the Judge to explain the delay. I was open and honest about everything, almost pleading for him to give me time to find them. I told him a mini-version of the most vicious assaults the pimps had perpetrated on the witnesses and that I feared for their safety and would be even more fearful if the accused were released and found them before I did. He could see I was gutted and eventually was sympathetic to my pleas. Despite the very verbal objections from the defence barristers, the Judge adjourned the case for 24 hours and told me to bring my witnesses to court. I was told by our prosecuting barrister that I had been very fortunate, as he'd never seen a Judge take that action before.

To my eternal regret, the next day I had to watch both men walk free. The more evil of the two grinned at me and drew his finger across his throat, in a gesture of cutting my throat, as he left the dock. My colleagues had to physically hold me back.

Three months later, with still no sign of the girls, I was summoned into the Detective Chief Superintendent's office and told I had to stop harassing the evil pimp. He showed me a letter from the pimp's solicitor making a complaint about me. In it he stated that his client was frightened whenever he saw me staring at him in the pubs and clubs in the red light area. It indicated that a private prosecution would follow if I didn't behave as a police officer should. I told the Chief Super that that was how real policemen should behave under the circumstances. It's hard to explain the depth of my anger, my disappointment and my feelings, but even I knew that when a Chief Superintendent told you not to do something you had to obey. It was a tough instruction to follow, and much harder to swallow.

My girls eventually surfaced working as prostitutes in Norwich about a year later, under false names. One of them – I think from his description the one who had started the ball rolling for me —asked one of the Norwich Vice Squad officers to call me to let me know they were all safe, without giving him her real name. He was good enough to make the call and after I'd spoken to him, also good enough not question her further about her comments or her identity. He asked me if I wanted to speak with her, but I said no and thanked him for the call. Even though they were back to working as prostitutes, I consoled myself that at least they were alive and their pimps had lost nine months of their lives on remand. And my time would come, I told myself almost daily.

As it happened, against all my willpower, that time didn't come, but at least both pimps left Bradford to live and work in Manchester. Work as criminals of course, not the work the rest of us aspire to. I was feared and respected by many criminals, but I felt defeated, or at least deflated, for a long time afterwards.

I suppose I could carry on with many more stories and incidents of my life as an enthusiastic copper, but having just re-read my account of those bastard pimps, my enthusiasm has dimmed a bit. I think if I spend time reflecting on my failure to send them to prison, I'll end up never going back to my memoirs and therefore not achieving my ambition of enjoying writing — and finishing — them. A bit of a sad note to end on, but I hope you've enjoyed my memoirs and appreciate why I'm drawing a line under it now. Bring back the seventies!

59

AND FINALLY

■▼■▼■▼■▼■▼■▼■▼■▼■▼■▼■

I will summarise the next few years; quickly, because it has nothing to do with these police memoirs. There were plenty of policing years ahead of me, but promotion dulls the enthusiasm for adventure and it seems we all start to think about pensions, or at least security.

In the words of my Amazonian wife, I chose my children over a successful marriage to her, and a lot of it was true. How can I blame my dad for that? I seem to recall a long time ago my first wife accusing me of choosing the job over a successful marriage to her.

I often looked back at my 70s mantra 'Erections rule OK!' I wonder, if they hadn't ruled, would my children have been brought up by two happily-married parents. Of course I'm not foolish enough to believe it was only my erections that were at fault. Of course I can't totally blame my previous wives for erections ruling, but I'm happy to offer to share some of the blame if you understand what I mean.

I hope your memories of my memoirs are not mainly about sex and erections. The memories I've written down probably account for about two percent of my life in the police. I helped countless women, young and old, who were abused, and had a meaningful relationship with only one, my Beautiful Swan. That relationship was very memorable, and I have few regrets.

Have I enjoyed writing my memoirs? It has certainly been cathartic – apart from that last bit about the bastard pimps. Perhaps I should delete that section. I know those poor girls feared not just for their safety, but for their very lives. Even if their pimps had rightly languished behind bars, they had fellow pimps who would have been only too delighted to take control over 'their' girls. And their punishment to create compliance would have been too horrible for them to contemplate. I understand, and just in case you are still around and reading this, good luck and I wish you well.

Anyway, writing all this down has certainly helped me come to terms with some of my demons, so that's good. I can clearly see the downside I created for others, but I never said I was perfect. It's been a selfish 'write' of passage really, with just random highlights that it suits me to write about. I could have been more detailed and specific in my recollection, and written things to please others. I could have written a book based solely on the 'good' things I did during my service, but that would have been a penance rather than a pleasure. Obviously I'm not as altruistic as I thought I was. I've hurt a lot of people, mentally and physically, during my police career, but I've made far, far more people happier and I'm sure, enhanced many others' lives in the process. If I wrote a thousand more pages you'd probably think most of my time as a serving police officer did a lot more good than harm. Honestly!

My stutter is long gone and I can now recite Stanley Holloway's *The Lion and Albert* from memory in front of any kind of audience, without a falter in sight. What more does a man want?

Should I let people read this? I'm vacillating here, because selfishly I want people to read my memoirs and say they've enjoyed them – of course I do. One thing is for sure though, I feel much better for writing them. I'm sober, respectful of others, married for the third time, and totally content. (As my third best man said in his wedding speech, my marriage to Karen is a 'triumph of hope over experience'). I've never beaten any of my wives and it's a shame that I should even have to mention it. I've been very lucky to have lived the life I've got away with, with only a few regrets, over many exciting and politically incorrect years.

Should I send this book to a newspaper in New Zealand in the hope that they publish it and Nancy reads it and forgives me, or is it time to draw a line under that now?

Am I happily married at last? You bet I am. Karen is a beautiful, intelligent, loving Geordie; a redhead, born under Leo the Lion, to parents of Irish and Scottish blood, and not to be argued with. Just what I've always wanted – or needed. She's had the good sense to move on from her other husbands and make me her third and final one. Karen's inherited her family's historical determination, passion and fiery attitude to fight when she believes justice is required. We share that ideal. She's loyal, loving and forgiving and very supportive. But she hasn't read this yet. She keeps popping in and asking me what I'm typing. Karen, I hope you read this before you read my obituary! I live in hope, continuing to make memories, as always.

Karen is the final piece in my jigsaw of a life – and I've discovered I love monogamy. I know, but if I'd found it before, I wouldn't have met her!

Thanks for reading my memoirs. They are the truth, the whole truth and nothing but the truth.